W9-BXP-163

JAMES

WALKING THE TALK

AT A GLANCE

UNIT	REFERENCE	SUBJECT	PAGE
1	James 1:1	Background to the Letter	12
2	James 1:2–11	Trials and Temptations	16
3	James 1:12–18	Testing	20
4	James 1:19–27	Listening and Doing	24
5	James 2:1–13	Favoritism Forbidden	28
6	James 2:14–26	Faith and Deeds	32
7	James 3:1–12	Taming the Tongue	36
8	James 3:13–18	Two Kinds of Wisdom	40
9	James 4:1–12	Submit Yourselves to God	44
10	James 4:13–17	Boasting About Tomorrow	48
11	James 5:1–6	Warning to Rich Oppressors	52
12	James 5:7–12	Patience in Suffering	56
13	James 5:13–20	The Prayer of Faith	60

Serendipity House / P.O. Box 1012 / Littleton, CO 80160

TOLL FREE 1-800-525-9563 / www.serendipityhouse.com

© 1988, 1998 Serendipity House. All rights reserved.

99 00 01 / **301 series • CHG** / 4

PROJECT ENGINEER:
Lyman Coleman

WRITING TEAM:
Richard Peace, Lyman Coleman, Andrew Sloan, Cathy Tardif

PRODUCTION TEAM:
Christopher Werner, Sharon Penington, Erika Tiepel

COVER PHOTO:
© Copyright International by Robert Cushman Hayes, All Rights Reserved

CORE VALUES

Community:	The purpose of this curriculum is to build community within the body of believers around Jesus Christ.
Group Process:	To build community, the curriculum must be designed to take a group through a step-by-step process of sharing your story with one another.
Interactive Bible Study:	To share your "story," the approach to Scripture in the curriculum needs to be open-ended and right brain—to "level the playing field" and encourage everyone to share.
Developmental Stages:	To provide a healthy program in the life cycle of a group, the curriculum needs to offer courses on three levels of commitment: (1) Beginner Stage—low-level entry, high structure, to level the playing field; (2) Growth Stage—deeper Bible study, flexible structure, to encourage group accountability; (3) Discipleship Stage—in-depth Bible study, open structure, to move the group into high gear.
Target Audiences:	To build community throughout the culture of the church, the curriculum needs to be flexible, adaptable and transferable into the structure of the average church.

ACKNOWLEDGMENTS

To Zondervan Bible Publishers
for permission to use
the NIV text,
The Holy Bible, New International Bible Society.
© 1973, 1978, 1984 by International Bible Society.
Used by permission of Zondervan Bible Publishers.

WELCOME TO THE SERENDIPITY 301 DEPTH BIBLE STUDY SERIES

You are about to embark on an adventure into the powerful experience of depth Bible Study. The Serendipity 301 series combines three basic elements to produce a life-changing and group-changing course.

First, you will be challenged and enriched by the personal Bible Study that begins each unit. You will have the opportunity to dig into Scripture both for understanding and personal reflection. Although some groups may choose to do this section together at their meeting, doing it beforehand will greatly add to the experience of the course.

Second, you will benefit from the group sessions. Wonderful things happen when a small group of people get together and share their lives around the Word of God. Not only will you have a chance to take your personal study to a deeper level, you will have an opportunity to share on a deep level what's happening in your life and receive the encouragement and prayer support of your group.

Third, the 301 courses provide the stimulus and tools for your group to take steps toward fulfilling your group mission. Whether or not your group has gone through the preparation of a Serendipity 101 and 201 course, you can profit from this mission emphasis. The 32-page center section of this book will guide you through this process. And questions in the closing section of the group agenda will prompt your group to act upon the mission challenge to "give birth" to a new small group.

Put these three components together, and you have a journey in Christian discipleship well worth the effort. Enjoy God's Word! Enjoy genuine Christian community! Enjoy dreaming about your mission!

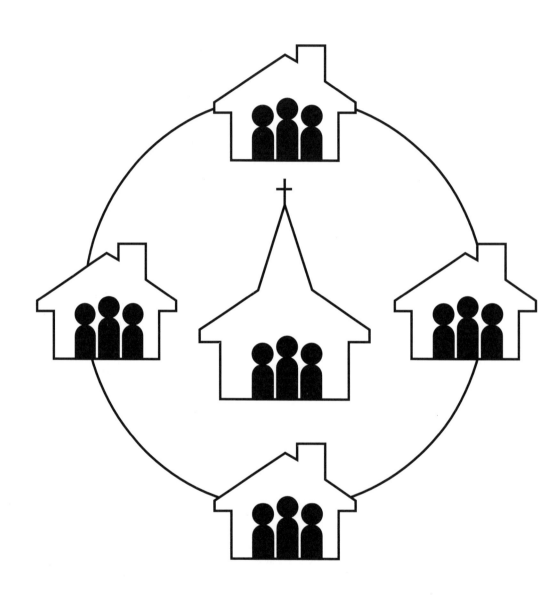

QUESTIONS & ANSWERS

STAGE

1. What stage in the life cycle of a small group is this course designed for?

Turn to the first page of the center section of this book. There you will see that this 301 course is designed for the third stage of a small group. In the Serendipity "Game Plan" for the multiplication of small groups, your group is in the Release Stage.

GOALS

2. What are the goals of a 301 study course?

As shown on the second page of the center section (page M2), the focus in this third stage is heavy on Bible Study and Mission.

BIBLE STUDY

3. What is the approach to Bible Study in this course?

This course involves two types of Bible Study. The "homework" assignment fosters growth in personal Bible Study skills and in personal spiritual growth. The group study gives everyone a chance to share their learning and together take it to a deeper level.

SELF STUDY

4. What does the homework involve?

There are three parts to each assignment: (1) READ—to get the "bird's-eye view" of the passage and record your first impressions; (2) SEARCH—to get the "worm's-eye view" by digging into the passage verse-by-verse with specific questions; and (3) APPLY— to ask yourself, after studying the passage, "What am I going to do about it?"

THREE-STAGE LIFE CYCLE OF A GROUP

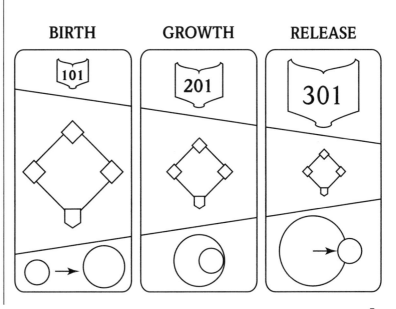

BIRTH   GROWTH   RELEASE

BIBLE KNOWLEDGE

5. *What if you don't know very much about the Bible?*

No problem. The homework assignment is designed to lead you step-by-step in your study. And there are study notes in each unit to give you help with key words, concepts and difficult passages.

AGENDA

6. *What is the agenda for the group meetings?*

The completed homework assignment becomes the basis for the group sharing. (However, those who don't do the homework should definitely be encouraged to come to the meeting anyway.) During the meeting the group will be guided to share on three levels: (1) TO BEGIN; (2) TO GO DEEPER; and (3) TO CLOSE.

STAYING ON TRACK

7. *How can the group get through all the material?*

Following the recommended time limits for each of the three sections will help keep you on track. Since you may not be able to answer all the questions with the time you have, you may need to skip some of them. Also, if you have more than seven people at a meeting, use the "Fearless Foursomes" described below for the Bible Study.

THE FEARLESS FOURSOME!

If you have more than seven people at a meeting, Serendipity recommends you divide into groups of 4 for the Bible Study. Count off around the group: "one, two, one, two, etc."—and have the "ones" move quickly to another room for the Bible Study. Ask one person to be the leader and follow the directions for the Bible Study time. After 30 minutes, the Group Leader will call "Time" and ask all groups to come together for the Caring Time.

GROUP BUILDING

8. *How does this course develop Group Building?*

Although this series is Serendipity's deepest Bible Study curriculum, Group Building is still essential. The group will continue "checking in" with each other and will challenge each other to grow in Christian discipleship. Working together on the group's mission should also be a very positive group-building process.

**MISSION /
MULTIPLICATION**

9. *What is the mission of a 301 group?*

Page M3 of the center section summarizes the mission of groups using this course: to commission a team from your group to start a new group. The center section will lead your group in doing this.

**LEADERSHIP
TRAINING**

10. *How do we incorporate this mission into the course?*

Page M5 of the center section gives an overview of the six steps in this process. You can either add this leadership training to the sessions a little bit at a time or in a couple of separate sessions.

**GROUP
COVENANT**

11. *What is a group covenant?*

A group covenant is a "contract" that spells out your expectations and the ground rules for your group. It's very important that your group discuss these issues—preferably as part of the first session (also see page M32 in the center section).

**GROUND
RULES**

12. *What are the ground rules for the group?* (Check those that you agree upon.)

❐ PRIORITY: While you are in the course, you give the group meetings priority.

❐ PARTICIPATION: Everyone participates and no one dominates.

❐ RESPECT: Everyone is given the right to their own opinion and all questions are encouraged and respected.

❐ CONFIDENTIALITY: Anything that is said in the meeting is never repeated outside the meeting.

❐ EMPTY CHAIR: The group stays open to new people at every meeting as long as they understand the ground rules.

❐ SUPPORT: Permission is given to call upon each other in time of need—even in the middle of the night.

❐ ADVICE GIVING: Unsolicited advice is not allowed.

❐ MISSION: We agree to do everything in our power to start a new group as our mission (see center section).

INTRODUCTION TO THE BOOK OF JAMES

By comparison with other New Testament books, James is an oddity. Stylistically, it is quite different. The way it is written is more akin to the book of Proverbs than to the epistles of Paul, much less to any of the Gospels. But even more than its style, the content of James sets it apart. In many ways, what is unique about James is not what it says, but what it does not say. James does not talk about most of the themes we have come to expect in the New Testament. Instead, James sets out in its own direction.

So, in James you will find no mention of the Holy Spirit and no reference to the redemptive work of Christ nor even to his resurrection. In fact, there are only two references to the name Jesus Christ (1:1 and 2:1). Furthermore, when examples are given, they are drawn from the lives of Old Testament prophets, not from the experience of Jesus. The title "Lord" does appear 11 times but generally it refers to God and not to Jesus. Indeed, it is God the Father who is the focus in the book of James.

For this reason, Martin Luther wrote that:

St. John's Gospel and his first epistle, St. Paul's epistles, especially Romans, Galatians and Ephesians, and St. Peter's first epistle are the books that show Christ and teach you all that is necessary and salvatory for you to know, even if you were never to see or hear any other book or doctrine. Therefore St. James' epistle is really an epistle of straw, compared to these others, for it has nothing of the nature of the gospel about it.

But Luther notwithstanding, James is clearly a Christian piece of writing, full of wisdom, solidly based on the teachings of Jesus, and a genuine product of first-century Christianity. To be sure, it is not as directly theological as many other New Testament epistles, but then James' concern is not doctrine (which he seems to assume). Rather, it is ethics—how the Christian faith is to be lived out on a day-by-day basis. As Johann Gottfried Herder wrote, "If the Epistle is 'of straw,' then there is within that straw a very hearty, firm, nourishing ... grain."

Authorship

In the New Testament there are apparently four men by the name of James, but only two who conceivably might have written this epistle—either James the apostle or James the Just, the half-brother of Jesus. Since it is almost certain that James the apostle (the son of Zebedee) was killed by Herod in A.D. 44 (before the epistle could have been written), traditionally the author has been assumed to be James, the leader of the church in Jerusalem and the brother of Jesus (Mark 6:3).

James' relationship to Jesus is not totally clear, however, apart from the fact that they are closely related. Some maintain that they were cousins (the New Testament word for "brother" is looser in meaning than the modern equivalent). Robert Gundry thinks James might have been ...

... an older stepbrother of Jesus by a (conjectural) marriage of Joseph previous to his marriage to Mary. The latter view, which excludes any blood relationship to Jesus, might better explain the failure of Jesus' brother to believe in Him during His lifetime (Mark 3:21, John 7:2–8); and a lack of concern for Mary because she was only their stepmother might also explain why Jesus from the cross, committed His mother to the apostle John (John 19:25–27). But the reason may have been that Mary's discipleship alienated her from her other children, who still did not believe in Jesus (*A Survey of the New Testament*, Robert H. Gundry, p. 324).

James and Jesus

If James, the author of this epistle, is really the brother of Jesus, why then doesn't he ever quote Jesus? This question has puzzled many people including the Latin Father, Jerome, and the church historian, Eusebius, both of whom comment on the fact that for this reason not everyone accepts this epistle as having been written by our Lord's brother.

But the problem is more apparent than real. In fact, James does quote Jesus once (5:12), even though he does not identify Jesus as the source of this statement. Furthermore, James alludes to Jesus' teaching regularly—"some 35 times in the epistle, or once every three verses (e.g., 2:5 and Matt. 5:3,5; 2:6 and Luke 18:3; 2:8 and Matt. 22:39–40)" (Davids, GNC).

We tend to miss the close connection between James and Jesus because we expect to find exact quotations taken from one of the written Gospels. But the early church did not have the written Gospels for the first 30 years of its existence. Their's was an oral tradition. In Hebrew school, even small children memorized large portions of the Old Testament—word for word. The whole educational system was based on memorization and so these Jewish Christians would have memorized the sayings of Jesus. They did not need a written text to know the words of Jesus. Thus, all James has to do is to allude to a saying of Jesus and his readers would catch the reference and remember the full statement by the Lord.

When we compare the book of James to the teachings of Jesus in the Sermon on the Mount (Matt. 5–7) and in the Sermon on the Plain (Luke 6), we begin to see how close the two are. We may look for quotations, but James gives us the very essence and spirit of his brother's teaching.

Style

Though written in epistle form, James seems more akin to Old Testament wisdom literature (like Proverbs) than to other New Testament letters. At first glance, it appears to be loosely structured and rambling in style. James seems to jump from one idea to another without any overall plan—except, perhaps, that of providing a manual of Christian conduct. A more detailed analysis reveals that the book of James is more like a sermon than anything else. It shares many characteristics of the sermonic style of both Greek philosophers and Jewish rabbis.

As in Greek sermons and synagogue homilies, James carries on a conversation with a hypothetical opponent (2:18–26; 5:13–16); switches subjects by means of a question (2:14; 4:1); uses a lot of commands (60 of the 108 verses in James are imperatives); relies on vivid images from everyday life (3:3–6; 5:7); illustrates points by reference to famous people (2:21–23, 25; 5:11,17); uses vivid antitheses in which the right way is set alongside the wrong way

(2:13,26); begins the sermon with a striking paradox that captures the hearers' attention (1:2 "consider it pure joy ... whenever you face trials"!); is quite stern at points (2:20; 4:4); and clinches a point by means of a quotation (1:11,17; 4:6; 5:11,20) (Ropes and Barclay). It should be noted, as William Barclay writes:

> The main aim of these ancient preachers, it must be remembered, was not to investigate new truth; it was to awaken sinners to the error of their ways, and to compel them to see truths which they knew but deliberately neglected or had forgotten (*The Letters of James and Peter*, pp. 33–34).

The best guess is that underlying the epistle of James are a series of sermons—preached by James—which were later edited into a "literary letter." A "literary letter" is written to be published rather than mailed to actual recipients (as were Paul's letters).

Outline

It was once thought that the epistle of James was a series of disconnected statements on the general theme of Christian conduct. The book was understood to consist of a number of moral truths and exhortations strung together like pearls on a string; each statement beautiful and complete in itself.

In recent years, however, scholars have shown that "James is far from a random collection of thoughts and sayings, but is a carefully constructed work" (Davids, NIGTC).

Specifically, it consists of an opening statement in which the three themes of the letter are stated twice (1:2–27). Then these three themes are explored in detail (2:1–5:6). The letter closes in the usual fashion (5:7–20). An outline of the books looks like this:

1. Greetings (1:1)
2. Introduction of Themes (1:2–27)
   A. First Statement: Testing, Wisdom, Wealth (1:2–11)
   B. Second Statement: Testing, Speech, Generosity (1:12–27)
3. Theme 1: Poverty and Generosity (2:1–26)

9

4. Theme 2: Wisdom and Speech (3:1–4:12)
5. Theme 3: Testing and Wealth (4:13–5:6)
6. Closing (5:7–20)*

*This outline follows the work of Peter Davids (NIGTC).

Notice that the first statement of the theme in 1:2–11 is not only recapitulated in the second statement of the theme (1:12–27), but expanded upon. Wisdom is now dealt with in terms of speech, and the issue of wealth becomes the question of generosity. Notice, too, that these three themes are approached in reverse order in the body of the text. In other words, far from a random collection of ideas, this is a carefully crafted piece of work.

Background
James draws his language, images and ideas from three worlds: early Christianity, Judaism and Greek culture. From Christianity he uses the language of eschatology (e.g., 5:7–9), common patterns of Christian ethical instructions which parallel those of 1 Peter (1:2–4,21; 4:7–10) and echo the teachings of Jesus (e.g., 1:5,17; 2:5,8,19; 4:3; 5:12). From Judaism, he draws his insistence on the unity of God, his concern for keeping the Law, and his quotations from Jewish Scriptures (2:8,11,21–25; 4:6; 5:11,17–18) along with the use of certain Jewish terms (e.g., hell is referred to as *Gehenna* in 3:6). From the Greek world—"the shared culture of the eastern Mediterranean area within the Roman Empire that resulted from the conquests of Alexander the Great" (Laws, *The Epistle of James*, p. 5)—he drew the language for the epistle (which he uses with remarkable skill), the source of his Old Testament quotes (he uses the Septuagint, the Greek Old Testament, not the Hebrew version of the Old Testament), Greek forms of composition, and metaphors drawn from the Greek and Latin sources (e.g., the horse and the ship in 3:3–4).

Special Concerns
While James clearly stands in the tradition of other Christian writers, he has some special concerns. The relationship between rich and poor is raised at various points (1:9–11; 2:1–7; 5:1–6)—

an issue of special significance to modern Western culture. He is also concerned about the use and abuse of speech (1:19,26; 2:12; 3:3–12; 5:12). He gives instruction on a special kind of speech—prayer (1:5–8; 4:2–3; 5:13–18). And he insists that endurance comes via testing (1:2–4,12–18; 5:7–11). Above all, he is concerned with ethical behavior. How believers act, he says, has eschatological significance—our future reward or punishment depends on it. In this regard, James bemoans the inconsistency of human behavior (1:6–8,22–24; 2:14–17; 4:1,3). Human beings are "double-minded" (1:8; 4:8), in sharp contrast to God who is one (2:19).

James has been taken by some (incorrectly) to be writing in reaction to Paul's doctrine of justification by faith (e.g., 2:14–26). In fact, if James had Paul in mind at all, he is addressing himself to those who had perverted Paul's message—insisting that it doesn't matter what you do as long as you have faith. James responds by asserting that works are the outward evidence to others of a claim to inner faith. In contrast, Paul is concerned with our standing before God. As is evident from Romans 12, Paul would certainly agree with James that faith in Christ has direct implications for how we live.

Destination
James, along with 1 and 2 Peter, John's three epistles and Jude, is one of the Catholic (or General) Epistles, so-called because it has no single destination. Thus it is not clear to whom James is addressing his comments. At first glance, it would appear that he is writing to Jewish Christians dispersed around the Greek world— "to the twelve tribes scattered among the nations" (1:1). But since Peter uses the same sort of inscription (1 Peter 1:1–2) and is clearly referring to Gentile Christians who consider themselves the New Israel, we are not sure for whom the book of James was intended. While the destination of the letter is unclear, the situation which sparked it is clear. The issues explained and discussed in the epistle fit what is known of the church in Jerusalem prior to its dispersion in A.D. 66.

Date

It is difficult to date the book of James. Some would place it very early, around A.D. 45, making it the first New Testament book. Others would date it quite late. However, the evidence seems to point increasingly to an early date. The sermons which are thought to underline this book would, of necessity, have been preached prior to James' death in A.D. 62. Furthermore, the seeming conflict with Paul's teaching—based on a misunderstanding of what Paul actually said—would have been resolved by A.D. 49 when Paul visited James in Jerusalem. So it seems that the oral part of the book, at least, dates from the middle to late 40s—some 12 to 15 years after the founding of the church.

Further Study

1. Read through James in one sitting. What characterizes his writing style? What concerns does James have? Check your conclusions with the previous material in this Introduction.

2. Compare the style of the book of James to that found in the letter written by the Council of Jerusalem in Acts 15:23–29.

3. Read through the Sermon on the Mount (Matt. 5–7), noting similarities to the book of James.

James: A Book for Sinners Like Us

Within the body of the New Testament, James is an unusual book with its almost total lack of "theology" (the theology is there but it's implicit) and its singleminded focus on behavior. Because of its special focus, we ought to pay the utmost attention to it, since it offers to us a rather penetrating glimpse both into the complexity of the human heart and the unpredictable nature of human behavior.

But James is not always easy to read. It can sound just like a series of moral platitudes—interesting, good for "other people," but not terribly gripping. However, there is a moment when James comes alive for us in a rather special way—when we are confronted with the experience of personal inadequacy, when we've acted inappropriately, when we've been the cause of problems or tensions, when our actions have been out of line. Without a sense of personal failure, it is all too easy to stand aloof from James' concerns: "I'm not like that. I'd never do that." But when we've "done that"—James provides for us both insight into the reasons for our failure and helpful (though not always easy) insights into what we should have done. At times like this, James is just the guide we need. At times like this, we gain invaluable insight into ourselves and learn yet another pointed lesson about what it means to follow Jesus. Without the book of James in the New Testament, we might never have gotten the point or learned the lesson. James is, indeed, a book for "sinners"—a book for us.

UNIT 1—Background to the Letter / James 1:1

1 *James, a servant of God and of the Lord Jesus Christ,*

To the twelve tribes scattered among the nations:

Greetings.

READ

Two readings of the passage are suggested—each with a response to be checked or filled in on the worksheet.

First Reading / First Impressions: To get familiar with the passage, read the passage through without stopping and record your "first impressions."

Read chapter one and check the box that comes the closest to the way the passage sounds to you.
- ❐ syndicated column / Ann Landers
- ❐ locker-room pep talk
- ❐ seminary professor
- ❐ sourpuss / killjoy
- ❐ boot camp Marine sergeant
- ❐ marriage counselor

Second Reading / Big Idea: To get the overall idea, thought or "gist" of the passage, read the passage slowly as though you are seeing the action from the press box—high above the stadium.

Read the first chapter again and check the box that best describes the "big idea" in the first chapter.
- ❐ I'm writing because I'm concerned for you.
- ❐ Get your act together.
- ❐ Shape up or ship out.
- ❐ Every day with Jesus is sweeter than the day before.
- ❐ You only go around once in life, so reach for the gusto.
- ❐ Tough times don't last but tough people do.
- ❐ Be good to yourself.
- ❐ You ought to be ashamed of yourself.

SEARCH

1. What is the situation when we first encounter James in the New Testament (Acts 15)?

2. How would you assess the character and concerns of James by the little you discover in this passage (Acts 15, especially verses 13–29)?

3. What do you suppose was the position of James in the church in Jerusalem and the early church in general (Acts 21:17–19; see also the note on "James" on page 14)?

4. How does James describe himself (James 1:1; see note)?

5. Who was this letter addressed to (v. 1; see notes)?

6. From a quick reading of the first chapter, how would you describe James' letter-writing style (see "Style" in the Introduction)?

7. From a quick scanning of the captions in the book of James, how would you describe his major concerns (see "Special Concerns" in the Introduction)?

APPLY
1. As you begin this course, what are some goals you would like to work on? Check one or two from the list below and add another if you wish.
   ❏ to get to know God in a more personal way
   ❏ to understand what I believe as a Christian and where I stand on issues
   ❏ to develop my skills in Bible study and personal devotions
   ❏ to belong to a small group that will support me in my growth
   ❏ to think through my values and priorities in light of God's will
   ❏ to wrestle with the next step in my spiritual journey with others who care

2. What are you willing to commit to in the way of disciplines during the time you are in this course?
   ❏ to complete the Bible study home assignment before the group meets
   ❏ to attend the group meetings except in cases of emergency
   ❏ to share in leading the group—taking my turn in rotation
   ❏ to keep confidential anything that is shared in the group
   ❏ to reach out to others who are not in a group and invite them to join us
   ❏ to participate in the group's mission of "giving birth" to a new group (see center section)

GROUP AGENDA

Every group meeting has three parts: (1) To Begin (10–15 minutes) to break the ice; (2) To Go Deeper (30 minutes) for Bible Study; and (3) To Close (15–30 minutes) for caring and prayer. When you get to the second part, have someone read the Scripture out loud and then divide into groups of 4 (4 at the dining table, 4 at the kitchen table, etc.). Then have everyone come back together for the third part.

TO BEGIN / 10–15 Min. (Choose 1 or 2)

1. When you were young, what adult most often gave you advice about growing up? How did you feel when that person wanted to talk with you?

2. What is one piece of wisdom that this person gave you that you still recall?

3. As you look back on "the good old days" in your life, were they more likely to be the hard times or the easy times?

TO GO DEEPER / 30 Min. (Choose 2 or 3)

1. From what you remember about the book of James and from your study in the "homework," how would you compare James to the apostle Paul?

2. What does the fact that there is so little doctrinal teaching in this letter say to you?

3. Why do you think James was so concerned about the things he wrote about in this book?

4. Did your decision to follow Christ have more to do with the example of Christian lives around you or a study of Christian beliefs?

5. CASE STUDY: Hard times have fallen on your community. Many of your friends are out of work, and some of the "rich" people in the church are "hoarding" their money. You just learned that your closest friends have lost their house and business. They are very discouraged. How would you handle this?

TO CLOSE / 15–30 Min.

1. How do you feel about seeing yourself as a "servant" (actually a "slave") of the Lord Jesus Christ?

2. What did you check in the first question in APPLY concerning the goals you would like to work on during this course?

3. What disciplines are you willing to commit to (second question in APPLY)?

4. How would you like this group to pray for you?

NOTES

Summary. James begins his letter in the same way most Greek letters began—by naming the sender and the recipient and then by offering a greeting. This is a letter from James the brother of Jesus (he is so well-known that he does not need further identification) to Jewish Christians living outside the region of Palestine.

1:1 *James*. "James" is the Greek version of the common Hebrew name "Jacob." As discussed in the "Authorship" section of the Introduction, this James is assumed to be the brother of Jesus who was known in the early church as "James the Just." The pilgrimage of James to faith is fascinating. At first, the family of Jesus, presumably including James, was hostile to Jesus' ministry (John 7:5) and, in fact, tried to stop it at one point (Mark 3:21). Yet following Jesus' ascension, Jesus' mother and brothers are listed among the early believers (Acts 1:14). For James, this coming to faith may have resulted from Jesus' postresurrection appearances to him (1 Cor. 15:7). In any case, James emerges as the leader of the church in Jerusalem. It is to James that Peter reports after his miraculous escape from Herod's prison (Acts 12:17). It is James who presides over the first Jerusalem Council, in which the important question is decided on whether to admit Gentiles to the church (Acts 15, esp. vv. 13–21). James is consulted by Paul during Paul's first trip to Jerusalem after his conversion (Gal. 1:19). Later, James joins in the official recognition of Paul's call as the Apostle to the Gentiles (Gal. 2:8–10). It is to James that Paul brings the collection for the poor (Acts 21:17–19). We also know that James was a strict Jew, adhering to Mosaic Law (Gal. 2:12). Yet he did back Paul's ministry to the Gentiles (Acts 21:17–26), unlike the Judaizers. Extrabiblical accounts tell us that James was martyred in A.D. 62. The high priest Annas the Younger seized James, who was then condemned and stoned to death. A few years later, in A.D. 66, the church in Jerusalem which James headed itself came to an end. Fearing the approaching Roman armies, the church members fled to Pella in the Transjordan and never returned to Jerusalem.

***a servant*.** James is so well-known that he needs no further designation. In fact, in the letter of Jude this wide recognition of James is used by the author to identify himself: "Jude, a servant of Jesus Christ and a *brother of James*." (In contrast, it is often necessary for Paul to identify himself as an apostle, thereby asserting his apostolic authority in the matters about which he is writing. See, for example, Romans 1:1 and 1 Corinthians 1:1). James' modest designation of himself as "a servant" instead of "Bishop of Jerusalem" or "the brother of Jesus" is probably a reflection of his genuine humility. Here he identifies Jesus as the "Lord" (master), so therefore the appropriate relationship of all others to Jesus is as servants (literally "slaves").

the twelve tribes. This is a term used in the Old Testament to refer to the nation of Israel, even after 10 of the 12 tribes were lost and never reconstituted following Israel's captivity by the Assyrians. In the New Testament, it came to be associated with the Christian church. Christians saw themselves as the new Israel (Rom. 4; 9:24–26; Phil. 3:3; 1 Peter 2:9–10).

scattered. The word is, literally, *diaspora* and was used by Jews to refer to those of their number living outside Palestine in the Gentile world. Here it probably refers to those Jewish Christians living outside Palestine (see 1 Peter 1:1).

COMMENTS
The Martyrdom of James "The Lord's Brother"
An Account of Eusebius, Bishop of Caesarea

When Paul appealed to Caesar and was sent to Rome by Festus, the Jews were disappointed of the hope in which they had devised their plot against him and turned their attention to James the Lord's brother, who had been elected by the apostles to the episcopal throne at Jerusalem. This is the crime that they committed against him. They brought him into their midst and in the presence of the whole populace demanded a denial of his belief in Christ. But when, contrary to all expectation, he spoke as he liked and showed undreamt-of fearlessness in the face of the enormous throng, declaring that our Savior and Lord, Jesus, was the Son of God, they could not endure his testimony any longer, since he was universally regarded as the most righteous of men because of the heights of philosophy and religion which he scaled in his life. So they killed him, seizing the opportunity for getting their own way provided by the absence of a government, for at that very time Festus had died in Judaea, leaving the province without governor or procurator. How James died has already been shown by the words quoted from Clement, who tells us that he was thrown from the parapet and clubbed to death. But the most detailed account of him is given by Hegesippus, who belonged to the first generation after the apostles. In his fifth book, he writes:

> Control of the Church passed to the apostles, together with the Lord's brother James, whom everyone from the Lord's time till our own has called the Righteous, for there were many Jameses, but this one was holy from his birth; he drank no wine or intoxicating liquor and ate no animal food; no razor came near his head; he did not smear himself with oil, and took no baths. He alone was permitted to enter the Holy Place, for his garments were not of wool but linen. He used to enter the Sanctuary alone, and was often found on his knees beseeching forgiveness for the people, so that his knees grew hard like a camel's from his continually bending them to worship of God and beseeching forgiveness for the people. Because of his unsurpassable righteousness he was called the Righteous and *Oblias*—in our language "Bulwark of the People, and Righteousness"—fulfilling the declarations of the prophets regarding him.

This account is taken from Eusebius' *An Ecclesiastical History* (2:23), written around A.D. 325, from a translation by G.A. Williamson (Penguin Books), pp. 99–103.

UNIT 2—Trials and Temptations / James 1:2-11

Trials and Temptations

²Consider it pure joy, my brothers, whenever you face trials of many kinds, ³because you know that the testing of your faith develops perseverance. ⁴Perseverance must finish its work so that you may be mature and complete, not lacking anything. ⁵If any of you lacks wisdom, he should ask God, who gives generously to all without finding fault, and it will be given to him. ⁶But when he asks, he must believe and not doubt, because he who doubts is like a wave of the sea, blown and tossed by the wind. ⁷That man should not think he will receive anything from the Lord; ⁸he is a double-minded man, unstable in all he does.

⁹The brother in humble circumstances ought to take pride in his high position. ¹⁰But the one who is rich should take pride in his low position, because he will pass away like a wild flower. ¹¹For the sun rises with scorching heat and withers the plant; its blossom falls and its beauty is destroyed. In the same way, the rich man will fade away even while he goes about his business.

READ

First Reading / First Impressions: What is your first impression of this passage?

❒ This is crazy.
❒ This is comforting.

❒ This is upside-down.
❒ This is reality.

Second Reading / Big Idea: Paraphrase what you think is the main verse or point here.

SEARCH

1. What is a Christian's attitude to be when facing trials (v. 2; also see notes)?

2. What is the purpose or value of testing (v. 3; also see notes)?

3. What is the ultimate goal of this process (v. 4; also see notes)?

4. If Christians cannot understand this process, what should they ask for (v. 5; also see notes)?

5. When Christians are going through storms, what do they need to guard against (vv. 6–8)?

6. How should Christians who happen to be poor look at themselves (v. 9; also see notes)?

7. How should those who happen to be rich think of themselves (v. 10; also see notes)?

8. What is the problem with wealth (v. 11)?

APPLY

From now on in the APPLY phase, you will be asked to try various forms of application. In this unit, try paraphrase. Go back and read verses 2–3—phrase by phrase. Close your eyes and try to restate the idea of a phrase in your own words—like you were explaining the thought to your next-door neighbor. Then, in the space below, write your own original expanded paraphrase of these verses. Include your own particular "trials" and struggles—at home, work, church, etc.

(EXAMPLE: I take comfort in the struggles I am going through at work, because I have faith that God will help me get through this and is preparing me for the future ...)

GROUP AGENDA

Every group meeting has three parts: (1) To Begin (10–15 minutes) to break the ice; (2) To Go Deeper (30 minutes) for Bible Study; and (3) To Close (15–30 minutes) for caring and prayer. When you get to the second part, have someone read the Scripture out loud and then divide into groups of 4 (4 at the dining table, 4 at the kitchen table, etc.). Then have everyone come back together for the third part.

TO BEGIN / 10–15 Min. (Choose 1 or 2)
1. What is the hardest test you can remember taking: Grade school test? College exam? Driver's test?

2. What do you do to cheer up when you're down in the dumps?

3. In your family, who does everyone lean on in hard times?

TO GO DEEPER / 30 Min. (Choose 2 or 3)
1. From the homework questions and the reference notes, what did you learn about what a Christian's attitude should be when facing trials?

2. How often is this *your* attitude when you are experiencing hard times?

3. What do you do when you are going through terrible hardships and you want to trust God's wisdom, but you still have doubts?

4. How does James turn upside-down the assumed status of rich and poor? How realistic is it for people to feel that way?

5. CASE STUDY: John grew up in an unstable home situation. He has experienced one failure after another. Recently, he was laid off at his job. He got drunk and lost his license. How would you deal with John?

TO CLOSE / 15–30 Min.
1. Who could you invite to this group next week?

2. How did you paraphrase verses 2–3 in the APPLY exercise?

3. On a scale from 1 (low) to 10 (high), what is the stress count in your life right now?

4. How can the group support you in prayer?

NOTES

Summary. James begins his book with a long introduction—the whole of chapter one—in which he lays out the three themes he will discuss. He uses what is called a "doubled opening": that is, he introduces his themes twice. So, in 1:2–11, he defines his three major themes for the first time: testing (vv. 2–4), wisdom (vv. 5–8), and riches (vv. 9–11). And then in 1:12–27 he reiterates these themes a second time. But in this second cycle James focuses on a slightly different aspect of each general theme: testing (vv. 12–18), speech (vv. 19–21), and generosity (vv. 22–27). The link between wisdom and speech, and between riches and generosity, will be made clear later in the book when these themes are explored in depth.

1:2–4 Here is the first theme James will treat in his book: the nature and value of trials and testing. This is a common theme in Christian ethical instruction (see Rom. 5:3–4 and 1 Peter 1:6–7). This theme is also found occasionally in the Old Testament(e.g., Gen. 22; Ps. 119:71 and the book of Job), though as Bacon remarked somewhat facetiously, "Prosperity is the blessing of the Old Testament, adversity the blessing of the New!"

1:2 *consider it pure joy.* James says that Christians ought to view the difficulties of life with enthusiasm because the outcome of trials will be beneficial. Such joy is not just a feeling. It is a form of activity. It is active acceptance of adversity.

my brothers. James is addressing his letter to those who are members of the church. This is not a letter for the world at large. The phrase "my brothers" carries with it a sense of warmth. Even though in the course of his letter James will say some very harsh things to these brothers and sisters, it is never with the sense that they are despised or even different from him (see 3:1–2). "My brothers" is a recurrent phrase in James, often used when a new subject is introduced (e.g., 1:2,19; 2:14; 3:1; 5:7).

trials of many kinds. The word "trials" has the dual sense of "adversity" on the one hand (e.g., lust, greed, trust in wealth)—i.e., "pleasant allurements of Satan or painful afflictions of the body (that) are apt to lead men to sin" (Adamson). James is not urging Christians to seek trials. Trials will come on their own. This is simply the way life is, especially, it seems, for a first-century Christian whose church is being persecuted.

1:3 One reason that the Christian can rejoice in suffering is because immediate good does come out of the pain. In this verse, James assumes that there will be good results.

perseverance. Or "endurance" (sticking it out). It is used in the sense of active overcoming, rather than passive acceptance. This is a virtue vital to the Christian life and comes mainly out of trials, it seems.

1:4 ***finish its work.*** Perfection is not automatic—it takes time and effort.

mature and complete. James has in mind here wholeness of character. He is not calling for some sort of esoteric perfection or sinlessness. Instead, what he seems to have in mind is moral blamelessness. He is thinking of the integrated life, in contrast to the divided person of verses 6–8. To be mature is to have reached a certain stage or to have fulfilled a given purpose. An animal had to be fully developed to be fit for sacrifice to God. To be complete is to have no flaws or blemishes. Once again this was a characteristic of the temple sacrifice.

lacking. The opposite of mature and complete. This is a word used of an army that has been defeated or a person who has failed to reach a certain standard.

1:5–8 Wisdom is needed in order to deal with trials so that they produce wholeness of character. Wisdom is needed to understand how to consider such adversity pure joy. Wisdom is the second theme which James will treat in his book.

1:5 ***wisdom.*** This is not just abstract knowledge, but rather God-given insight which leads to right living. It is the ability to make right decisions especially about moral issues, as one is called upon to do during trials.

generously. A reference both to the abundance of the gift and the spirit with which it is given. God gives fully, without hesitation and without grudging (see 2 Cor. 8:1–2).

ask God. See Matthew 7:7.

1:6 James now contrasts the lack of hesitation on God's part to give (v. 5) with the hesitation on people's part to ask (v. 6). Both here and in 4:3, unanswered prayer is connected to the quality of the asking, not to the unwillingness of God to give.

believe. To be in *one mind* about God's ability to answer prayer, to be sure that God will hear and will act in accord with his superior wisdom. The ability to pray this sort of trusting prayer is an example of the character which is produced by trials.

1:8 ***double-minded.*** To doubt is to be in *two minds*—to believe and to disbelieve simultaneously; to be torn between two impulses—one positive, one negative; epitomized perhaps by Augustine's prayer: "O Lord, grant me purity, but not yet" (see 4:8).

unstable. "The man who is divided in himself, then, will show himself as such in his doubtful prayer, and also in his inability to act firmly or reliably" (Laws).

1:9–11 Poverty is an example of a trial to be endured—but so too are riches, though in quite a different way. The question of riches and poverty is the third major theme in the book.

1:9 ***humble circumstances.*** Those who are poor in a material and social sense; those who have little and are looked down on by others because they are poor.

take pride. Such boasting is equivalent to the rejoicing that is encouraged in verse 2 in the face of adversity. Such an uncharacteristic attitude can only occur when the poor see beyond immediate circumstances to the fact of their new position as children of God. While they may be poor in worldly goods, they are rich beyond imagining since they are children of God and thus heirs of the whole world. Therefore, they do in fact have a superior position in life and ought to rejoice in it.

high position. In the early church, the poor gained a new sense of self-respect. Slaves found that traditional social distinctions had been obliterated (Gal. 3:28).

1:10 ***rich.*** The peril of riches is that people come to trust in wealth as a source of security. It is a mark of double-mindedness to attempt to serve both God and money. In James, the word rich "always indicates one outside the community, a nonbelieving person. The rich, in fact, are the oppressors of the community (2:6; 5:1–6)" (Davids, GNC).

low position. Jewish culture understood wealth to be a sure sign of God's favor. Here, as elsewhere (vv. 2,9), James reverses conventional expectations.

wild flower. In February, spring comes to Palestine with a blaze of color, as flowers like the lily, the poppy and the lupine blossom along with a carpet of grass. By May, however, all the flowers and grass are brown.

fade away. Wealth gives an uncertain security, since it is apt to be swept away as abruptly as desert flowers (see Isa. 40:6–8).

UNIT 3—Testing / James 1:12-18

¹²*Blessed is the man who perseveres under trial, because when he has stood the test, he will receive the crown of life that God has promised to those who love him.*

¹³*When tempted, no one should say, "God is tempting me." For God cannot be tempted by evil, nor does he tempt anyone;* ¹⁴*but each one is tempted when, by his own evil desire, he is dragged away and enticed.* ¹⁵*Then, after desire has conceived, it gives birth to sin; and sin, when it is full-grown, gives birth to death.*

¹⁶*Don't be deceived, my dear brothers.* ¹⁷*Every good and perfect gift is from above, coming down from the Father of the heavenly lights, who does not change like shifting shadows.* ¹⁸*He chose to give us birth through the word of truth, that we might be a kind of firstfruits of all he created.*

READ

First Reading / First Impressions: What are two or three key words here?

Second Reading / Big Idea: What's the main point or topic?

SEARCH

1. What is the promise for someone who perseveres under trial (v. 12)?

2. Who are we cautioned not to blame when we are tempted (v. 13; see notes)?

3. What is the source of temptation and how does it come about (v. 14)?

4. What are the downward steps to death and what do each mean (vv. 14–15; see notes)?

5. Instead of tempting us, what is God doing for us (v. 17)?

6. What can we be assured of—along with God's giving (v. 17)?

7. What is the gift of God and how did we learn about this gift (v. 18; see notes)?

APPLY
Meditate on verse 12—phrase by phrase—with your eyes closed. Then, rewrite the meaning of the verse in your own words. Next, record what this verse means to you. Finally, write out the verse (as it is) on a 3 x 5 card and put the card on your kitchen sink or on the dashboard of your car. Repeat this verse 7 times a day for 7 days—until you know the verse by memory.

GROUP AGENDA

Every group meeting has three parts: (1) To Begin (10–15 minutes) to break the ice; (2) To Go Deeper (30 minutes) for Bible Study; and (3) To Close (15–30 minutes) for caring and prayer. When you get to the second part, have someone read the Scripture out loud and then divide into groups of 4 (4 at the dining table, 4 at the kitchen table, etc.). Then have everyone come back together for the third part.

TO BEGIN / 10–15 Min. (Choose 1 or 2)

1. What sports team is your favorite underdog?

2. What "junk food" do you find most tempting: Cookies? Chips? French fries? Ice cream?

3. What special gift did you receive for Christmas in recent years?

TO GO DEEPER / 30 Min. (Choose 2 or 3)

1. Based on your study of this chapter, what would you say is the difference between trials and temptations? What is God's role in each?

2. From this passage, and from your own experience, what are the keys to resisting temptation?

3. Do you find it easy to blame someone else—either other people or God—for your mistakes?

4. What is one "good and perfect gift" (v. 17) that you are thankful for?

5. CASE STUDY: It all started with *Playboy*. Then X-rated movies. Now, your friend is trapped in an insatiable appetite for pornography. What is your advice?

TO CLOSE / 15–30 Min.

1. Has your group started on the six steps toward fulfilling your mission—from the center section?

2. What did you write in the APPLY exercise? Are you working on memorizing this verse?

3. What subtle enticement do you struggle with?

4. How can the group support you in prayer?

NOTES

Summary. James now reiterates his three themes for the second time. In this unit the subject is trials. James expands on what he said about trials in verses 2–4 by adding two more pieces of information. In verse 12 he tells us that trials bring blessedness, because out of them one receives the crown of life. (In verses 2–4 the emphasis was on the joy of testing because it brings maturity.) Then in verses 13–15 he looks at the source of failure during a trial. It is not God who is causing one to fail. Rather, it is one's own evil desire.

1:12 *Blessed.* Happy is he or she who has withstood all the trials to the end.

perseveres. In verse 3 James says that testing produces perseverance. Here he points out that such perseverance brings the reward of blessedness.

stood the test. Such a person is like metal which has been purged by fire and is purified of all foreign substances.

crown of life. As with Paul (Rom. 5:1–5) and Peter (1 Peter 1:6–7), James now focuses on the final result of endurance under trial: eternal life. Crowns were worn at weddings and feasts (and so signify joy); were given to the winner of an athletic competition (and so signify victory); and were worn by royalty (as befits children of God the King).

1:13–15 Perseverance under trial is not the only option. People can fail. In these verses James examines the causes of such failure.

1:13 *tempted.* The focus shifts from *enduring* outward trials (v. 12) to *resisting* inner temptations. Verse 12 is linked to verse 13 by a verbal echo: *peirasmos* (trial) in verse 12 and *perirazo* (temptation) in verse 13.

"God is tempting me." The natural tendency is to blame others for our failure. In this case, God is blamed for sending a test that was too hard to bear. That first-century Jewish Christians might reason in this fashion is probably a consequence of rabbinic teaching. Noting that human beings are double-minded and so inclined both toward good and toward evil, some rabbis concluded that in the same way that God was responsible for the positive side of human nature, he was also responsible for the evil side. One rabbinic saying reads: "God said, 'It repents me that I created the evil tendency in man ...!' " James stands opposed to this view. God does not put people into situations in order to test them.

Such temptations arise quite naturally from life itself. James will go on to say in verse 14 that what turns a natural situation into a temptation is evil desire within a person.

God cannot be tempted by evil. Though it is permissible to translate the Greek phrase this way, according to Davids, the better translation is: "God ought not to be tested by evil persons." "This meaning ... fits the grammar of the passage: *gar* introduces a cogent reason (God ought not to be tested: ipso facto you should cease from doing it) and *de* introduces a somewhat different reason (*he* does not test one anyway, so you are wrong in accusing him). Furthermore, this translation shows that James is drawing upon an important theme in Jewish theology: people in tight places tend to turn and challenge God, and they ought never to do so (for it is unfaith). The theme is summed up in the deuteronomic command, 'You shall not put the Lord your God to the test, as you tested him at Massah' (Deut. 6:16)" (Davids, NIGTC).

nor does he tempt anyone. God does not lure anyone into a tempting situation just to see whether that person will stand or fall. That is not God's nature. He does not desire evil nor cause evil.

1:14–15 The steps in temptation are explained by reference to the birth process ("conceived," "birth," "full-grown"). The possibility of an evil act is entertained, then acted on again and again (the thought becomes deed) until ultimately it brings death. In fact, the picture here is of a seductress who entices a victim into her bed, seduces him, and conceives a child whose name is *sin*. This child, in turn, produces his own offspring which is the monster called *death*. This same chain from desire to death is described by Paul in Romans 7:7–12.

1:14 *evil desire.* The true source of evil is a person's own inner inclination (Mark 7:21–23).

dragged away and enticed. A fishing image, "suggestive of a fish swimming in a straight course and then drawn off towards something that seems attractive, only to discover that the bait has a deadly hook in it" (Tasker).

1:15 The opposite of "the crown of life"; the point of no-return where a repeated act has become so ingrained that we have no ability to restrain ourselves.

1:16–18 God doesn't send the test; he sends the gift of wisdom to help us meet the trial. Far from tempting people, God gives gifts, most notably the gift of new life.

1:17 This is a line of Greek poetry, either original or a quotation from an unknown source.

Father of the heavenly lights. God is the creator of the stars.

shifting shadows. All created things, even stars, change and vary. God does not.

1:18 *birth.* The contrast is made between sin which gives birth to death and the Gospel (the word of truth) which gives birth to life and brings into being God's children.

firstfruits. At the beginning of the harvest, the earliest produce was offered to God as a symbol that the whole harvest was his.

UNIT 4—Listening and Doing / James 1:19-27

Listening and Doing

[19]*My dear brothers, take note of this: Everyone should be quick to listen, slow to speak and slow to become angry,* [20]*for man's anger does not bring about the righteous life that God desires.* [21]*Therefore, get rid of all moral filth and the evil that is so prevalent and humbly accept the word planted in you, which can save you.*

[22]*Do not merely listen to the word, and so deceive yourselves. Do what it says.* [23]*Anyone who listens to the word but does not do what it says is like a man who looks at his face in a mir-* ror [24]*and, after looking at himself, goes away and immediately forgets what he looks like.* [25]*But the man who looks intently into the perfect law that gives freedom, and continues to do this, not forgetting what he has heard, but doing it—he will be blessed in what he does.*

[26]*If anyone considers himself religious and yet does not keep a tight rein on his tongue, he deceives himself and his religion is worthless.* [27]*Religion that God our Father accepts as pure and faultless is this: to look after orphans and widows in their distress and to keep oneself from being polluted by the world.*

READ

First Reading / First Impressions: How do you feel reading this passage?

❑ condemned ❑ encouraged ❑ hopeless ❑ overwhelmed ❑ other:_____

Second Reading / Big Idea: How would this go over in the locker room of a professional hockey team?

SEARCH

1. What three specific behaviors does James command (v. 19; see notes)?

2. Why (v. 20)?

3. In what two ways are we to respond to this challenge (v. 21; see notes)?

4. What is the point James is making in verse 22?

5. What is the lesson in the metaphor about the mirror (vv. 23–24; see note)?

6. What is the promise for the person who continues in the "perfect law" (v. 25; see notes and Ps. 1)?

7. What is the ultimate test for someone who claims to be religious (v. 26)?

8. What are two concerns that any religious person should have (v. 27)?

APPLY
How would you evaluate yourself on the challenges James makes in this passage? Rate yourself on the following scales by placing an *"X"* on each line.

quick to listen, slow to speak	quick to speak, slow to listen
slow to become angry	quick to become angry
attentive to God's Word	neglectful of God's Word
compassionate toward the needy	callous toward the needy
unpolluted by the world	polluted by the world

GROUP AGENDA

After the first part, read the Scripture out loud and divide into groups of 4. Then come back together for the third part.

TO BEGIN / 10–15 Min. (Choose 1 or 2)

1. Are you better at talking or listening?

2. What "little thing" pushes your button—like squeezing the toothpaste tube in the middle?

3. Which best describes your temper: Short fuse, big bomb? Long fuse, little fizz? Long fuse, H-bomb? Can you give an example?

TO GO DEEPER / 30 Min. (Choose 2 or 3)

1. What is the difference between the anger James is writing about here and "righteous anger," like Jesus demonstrated when he cleansed the temple (Mark 11:15–17)?

2. Which type of anger do you express most often? How satisfied are you with the way you deal with anger?

3. How does the term "Sunday Christian" illustrate James' point in this passage?

4. Conversely, how does the "mirror" of God's Word effect change in a person's behavior?

5. In our world today, what does it mean to follow verse 27? In what way do you need to follow this verse more actively?

6. CASE STUDY: Your friend has a "short fuse" which always is getting her in trouble. And one of her children is just like her. Sparks fly ... and then they both feel terrible. What could you share from your own experience that would be of help?

TO CLOSE / 15–30 Min.

1. Has your group taken the survey for small groups in your church (see page M15 in the center section)? If so, what are you going to do as a result?

2. How did you respond to APPLY?

3. How can the group pray for you this week?

NOTES

Summary. In chapter one James twice introduces the three main subjects of his book. In this unit he identifies for the second time the second and third points he will discuss in his book: speech (vv. 19–21) and generosity (vv. 22–27).

1:19–21 Having just mentioned God's word (1:18), James shifts here to the subject of human words. From the "word of truth" he moves to the "word of anger." James is still, in fact, focusing on the theme of wisdom, except that now his concern is with the relationship between wisdom and speech—a connection he will make plainer in 3:1–4:12. James 1:6–8 parallels this section. There he pointed out that wisdom is a gift of God. Here he points out that the wise person is slow to speak.

1:19b The heart of what James wants to say is found in this proverb. This is not a new teaching. The Bible often commends the value of listening and the danger of too-hasty speech (see Prov. 10:19; 13:3; 17:28; 29:20; Matt. 12:36–37; James 3:1–12).

slow to speak. One needs to consider carefully what is to be said, rather than impulsively and carelessly launching into words that are not wise.

slow to become angry. James does not forbid anger. Repressed anger will eventually come out and then it can be quite destructive. Also, at times, anger is the only appropriate response to a situation. However, James does caution against responding in anger at every opportunity (see also Eccl. 7:9; Mark 11:15–17; Eph. 4:25–27,31; James 3:13–18).

1:20 This verse is reminiscent of what Jesus said in the Sermon on the Mount (Matt. 5:21-22). Human anger doesn't produce the kind of life that God wants.

1:21 If Christians are to speak wisely, they must prepare to do so by the dual action of ridding themselves of all that is corrupt and not of God and then by humbly relying upon the word of God which is within them already.

get rid of. This verb means literally, "to lay aside" or "to strip off" as one would do with filthy clothing. To be in tune with God's purpose first requires this negative action; this rejection or repentance of all that drags one down.

all moral filth and the evil. The two Greek words here refer to actual dirt and are used as a metaphor for moral uncleanness. Given the context, they probably refer primarily to vulgar and malicious speech (Laws).

humbly accept. Having renounced evil (a negative act) the next step is to accept that which is good (a positive act). This same twofold action of repentance and faith (rejecting evil and accepting God) is the path whereby people come to Christian faith in the first place. Repentance and faith are also the key to living out the Christian life. James has already twice mentioned the idea of receiving God's gifts (vv. 5,17). This receiving must be done humbly. This attitude contrasts directly with anger about which he just spoke.

the word. This is the same "word of truth" mentioned in verse 18. In contrast to the quick and angry words of people, words which hurt and destroy, there is the word of God which saves.

planted in you. They are Christians already. They have the life of God in them. It is now up to them to act upon what is already theirs. They must actualize in their lifestyles the truth of God.

1:22–27 The concept of *accepting* the word of God (v. 21) leads James to the concept of *doing* the word of God. Thus he moves from proper speech to proper action, which in this case is charity toward those in need. In this way he gets to his third theme, the idea that Christians are called upon to be generous in the face of poverty.

1:22 merely listen. The Christian must not just hear the word of God. A response is required.

deceive yourselves. It does not matter how well a person may know the teaching of the apostles or how much Scripture he or she has memorized. To make mere knowledge of God's will the sole criterion for the religious life is dangerous and self-deceptive.

Do what it says. This is James' main point in this section.

1:23–24 James illustrates his point with a metaphor. The person who reads Scripture (which is a mirror to the Christian, because in it his or her true state is shown) and then goes away unchanged is like the person who gets up in the morning and sees how dirty and disheveled they are, but then promptly forgets about it when the proper response would be to get cleaned up.

1:25 In contrast is the person who not only acts to correct what is discovered to be wrong, but then goes on acting in this way.

the perfect law. The reference is probably to the teachings of Jesus which set one free, in contradistinction to the Jewish Law which brought bondage (see Rom. 8:2).

blessed. The sheer act of keeping this "law" is a happy experience in and of itself because it produces good fruit, now and in the future.

1:26–27 In these verses James sums up what he has said in chapter one by way of introduction to his book. He says that the mark of the true Christian is, first, the ability to control the tongue (the theme of speech and wisdom); second, the willingness to engage in acts of charity (the theme of generosity in the face of poverty and wealth); and, third, the attempt to overcome the trials and temptations offered by the world (the theme of testing).

1:26 considers himself. The focus is on a person's own self-assessment of his or her religious commitment. In contrast, in verse 27, James tells us what God considers as truly religious.

religious. The emphasis here is probably on the overt acts of religion such as scrupulous observance of the details of worship and personal acts of piety.

a tight reign on his tongue. It is interesting that the inability to control one's speech is the mark of the person who thinks he or she is religious but in reality is not.

1:27 Religion. True religion actually has more to do with acts of charity than acts of piety. It involves caring for others and avoiding the corruption of one's culture.

orphans and widows. In the Old Testament the orphans and widows are the poor and oppressed whom God's people are to care for because God cares for them (see Deut. 10:17–18; 14:29; 24:17–22). A child without the protection and provision of parents is at the mercy of the community. So too is the widow who typically had an insecure place in ancient society. She had a certain social stigma to overcome, because for a man to die before he was old was considered a judgment on his sin and this disgrace was extended to his widow. A widow also found it difficult to support herself given the social situation of the times.

polluted. Unstained, pure, undefiled.

world. The Greek word is *kosmos* and refers to the world system that is in opposition to and at war with God (see John 15:18–25; 16:33; Rom. 12:2; 1 Cor. 2:12; James 4:4).

UNIT 5—Favoritism Forbidden / James 2:1-13

Favoritism Forbidden

2 My brothers, as believers in our glorious Lord Jesus Christ, don't show favoritism. ²Suppose a man comes into your meeting wearing a gold ring and fine clothes, and a poor man in shabby clothes also comes in. ³If you show special attention to the man wearing fine clothes and say, "Here's a good seat for you," but say to the poor man, "You stand there" or "Sit on the floor by my feet," ⁴have you not discriminated among yourselves and become judges with evil thoughts?

⁵Listen, my dear brothers: Has not God chosen those who are poor in the eyes of the world to be rich in faith and to inherit the kingdom he promised those who love him? ⁶But you have insulted the poor. Is it not the rich who are exploiting you? Are they not the ones who are dragging you into court? ⁷Are they not the ones who are slandering the noble name of him to whom you belong?

⁸If you really keep the royal law found in Scripture, "Love your neighbor as yourself,"ᵃ you are doing right. ⁹But if you show favoritism, you sin and are convicted by the law as lawbreakers. ¹⁰For whoever keeps the whole law and yet stumbles at just one point is guilty of breaking all of it. ¹¹For he who said, "Do not commit adultery,"ᵇ also said, "Do not murder."ᶜ If you do not commit adultery but do commit murder, you have become a lawbreaker.

¹²Speak and act as those who are going to be judged by the law that gives freedom, ¹³because judgment without mercy will be shown to anyone who has not been merciful. Mercy triumphs over judgment!

ᵃ8 Lev. 19:18   ᵇ11 Exodus 20:14; Deut. 5:18
ᶜ11 Exodus 20:13; Deut. 5:17

READ

First Reading / First Impressions: What type of preacher do you imagine James was?

❐ the pound-on-the-pulpit type   ❐ the stern, authoritarian type

❐ the win-them-with-love type   ❐ other:_____

Second Reading / Big Idea: How would you paraphrase what you see as the key verse here?

SEARCH

1. What issue does James take up here as an example of "religion ... pure and faultless" (1:27)?

2. What is the difference in the attire of the poor man and the rich man (v. 2)?

3. How is discrimination shown (vv. 3–4)?

4. What two gifts does God give to the poor (v. 5)?

5. What three things do the rich do to the poor (vv. 6–7; see notes)?

6. What is the royal law (v. 8; see notes)?

7. How does favoritism contradict this law (v. 9)?

8. Who are the lawbreakers (vv. 10–11; see note)?

9. What is the solution to the problem of favoritism and discrimination (vv. 12–13)?

APPLY

From this passage, it would be awfully easy to get very negative about things in the church. The fact is, we will never remove all favoritism or discrimination until we remove the "old nature." So instead of majoring only on the negative, take this opportunity to affirm what you have observed your church do to *overcome* favoritism (e.g., parking spaces reserved for visitors, people don't care how others dress, etc.). First, jot down some affirmations in this regard. Second, write down what you see as the message of this passage for your church today.

GROUP AGENDA

After the first part, read the Scripture out loud and divide into groups of 4. Then come back together for the third part.

TO BEGIN / 10–15 Min. (Choose 1 or 2)

1. Where do you sit in church? For what sporting or musical event would you buy the "best seats"?

2. Have you ever visited a country where there are only two classes—rich and poor?

3. When have you felt out of place because of the clothes you were wearing?

TO GO DEEPER / 30 Min. (Choose 2 or 3)

1. Do you think we have as much of a problem in our country with class discrimination in the church as in the countries where there is no middle class?

2. What is the principle on which to challenge discrimination in the church in any form?

3. Based on your study of this passage and the reference notes, what were the rich doing to the poor (vv. 6–7)? Does this happen today?

4. What is a Christian's responsibility in situations of social injustice?

5. Have you ever been the victim of discrimination in the secular world? In the church?

6. What does this passage say to you about your own conscious or unconscious treatment of others?

TO CLOSE / 15–30 Min.

1. Are you working on your mission as a group? Are you inviting new people to join you?

2. If a filthy homeless person came to your church or this group, how would they be treated?

3. What did you write in the APPLY exercise?

4. How would you like prayer for your church? How would you like prayer for yourself?

NOTES

Summary. James now begins his exposition of his first theme: poverty and generosity (2:1–26). Notice that he treats these themes in the reverse order from which he presented them in his introduction. In this chapter his focus is on the question of the rich and the poor. Christians are to have a different ethic than that of the world. They are not to favor the wealthy simply because they are wealthy, nor are they to despise the poor simply because they are poor. The poor are to be welcomed and aided. In fact, one's faith is shown by acts of generosity to the poor. The first half of the chapter (2:1–13) focuses on a warning against prejudice.

2:1–9 James' point is quite straightforward: to discriminate between people is inconsistent with the Christian faith. This is another example of how Christian faith must be expressed in right behavior.

2:1 James appeals to them "as believers in our glorious Lord Jesus Christ" not to discriminate. His reason is that Jesus alone is the "glorious Lord." There is only one Lord and he saves both rich and poor on the same basis—belief in him. Rich and poor are alike before their common Lord.

glorious. Jesus is described here by means of a word that denotes the presence of God. When God draws near, what people experience is the light of his splendor (see Ex. 16:10; 2 Chron. 7:1–3; Ezek. 8:4; Mark 9:2–7 and Luke 2:9). James' point is that in Jesus one sees a manifestation of God's presence.

favoritism. This is the act of paying special attention to someone because he or she is rich, important, famous, powerful, etc. Such discrimination (respect of persons) is condemned throughout Scripture (see Mal. 2:9; Acts 10:34–48; Rom. 2:11; Eph. 6:9 and Col. 3:25).

2:2–4 James now gives a specific example of how deference to the rich operates in the church. The situation he describes could well have happened in the first-century church. It was one of the few institutions where traditional social barriers had been dropped. It would have been quite possible for a wealthy landowner to belong to the same Christian assembly as one of his slaves. Peter Davids thinks that what James is describing is not a worship service but a judicial assembly in which the church has gathered to hear a dispute between two Christians, one rich and one poor (see 1 Cor. 6:1–11 for information about such matters).

2:2 *a gold ring.* This is the mark of those who

belonged to the equestrian order—the second level of Roman aristocracy. These noblemen were typically wealthy. Rings in general were a sign of wealth. The more ostentatious would fill their fingers with rings. Early Christians were urged to wear only one ring, on the little finger, bearing the image of a dove, fish or anchor.

fine clothes. These are literally "bright and shining" garments, like those worn by the angel in Acts 10:30.

poor man. The word used here denotes a beggar, a person from the lowest level of society. Had this been a low-paid worker a different Greek word would have been used.

shabby clothes. In contrast to the spotless garments of the rich man, the beggar wears filthy rags, probably because this is all the clothes he owns.

2:4 James condemns this behavior on two grounds. First, they are making distinctions between people when, in fact, Christ came to remove all such barriers (Gal. 3:28). Second, they are prejudicing their judicial decision in favor of the rich person and not listening only to the merits of the case.

2:4–7 James attacks this kind of discrimination. All social distinctions are null and void in the church. Partiality is clearly out of place. Both rich and poor are to be received equally. Notice that the rich are not condemned here, *per se*. They are welcome in the church. What is condemned is the insult to the poor (v. 6).

2:5 *those who are poor.* The New Testament is clearly on the side of the poor. In Jesus' first sermon he declared that he was called to preach the Gospel to the poor (Luke 4:18). When John the Baptist questioned whether Jesus was actually the Messiah, in response Jesus pointed to his preaching to the poor (Matt. 11:4–5). The poor are called blessed (Luke 6:20). The poor flocked to Jesus during his ministry and later into his church (1 Cor. 1:26). As William Barclay wrote, "It is not that Christ and the Church do not want the great and the rich and the wise and the mighty ... but it was the simple fact that the gospel offered so much to the poor and demanded so much from the rich, that it was the poor who were swept into the church."

2:6 *you have insulted the poor.* The Old Testament also condemns this behavior (see Prov. 14:21).

exploiting you. In a day of abject poverty the poor were often forced to borrow money at exorbitant rates of interest just to survive. The rich profited from their need.

dragging you into court. This was probably over the issue of a debt. "If a creditor met a debtor on the streets, he could seize him by the neck of his robe, nearly throttling him and literally drag him to the law courts" (Barclay).

2:7 Jesus levels a third charge at the rich. Not only do they exploit the poor and harass them in court, they also mock the name of Jesus. This would not be unexpected since the church was largely a collection of poor people and thus would be the object of scorn by the wealthy.

the noble name. The early followers of Jesus were dubbed with the name "Christians" (Acts 11:26). At baptism they formally took upon themselves the name of Christ, knowing that they might well be vilified simply for bearing that name.

2:8–9 Jesus drives home his point by citing Scripture.

2:8 *really keep.* Possibly James is here countering an argument that said that in treating the rich this way they were simply obeying the law of love. His point is that if they are really loving their neighbor (and not just his wealth) they would treat the poor with equal respect.

the royal law. James points to what Jesus called "the most important" commandment by which he summed up all of the Old Testament Law. This law of love is the central moral principle by which Christians are to order their lives (see Mark 12:28–33).

2:9 Favoritism is no light matter. James bluntly says that it is sin and it is lawbreaking.

2:10–11 Favoritism is not just transgression of a single law. In fact, it makes one answerable to the whole Law. The Jews thought of law-keeping in terms of credit and debit: did your good deeds outweigh your bad? In contrast, James says that breaking even one law (as everyone does) makes a person a lawbreaker and thus liable for judgment.

2:12–13 The idea of *judgment* is connected to the need for *mercy*. In fact, what James is calling for in verses 2–3 is mercy for the poor. Christians are not bound by rigid laws by which they will one day be judged, as Judaism taught. So the fear of future punishment is not a deterrent to behavior. Rather, it is the inner compulsion of love that motivates the Christian to right action.

UNIT 6—Faith and Deeds / James 2:14-26

Faith and Deeds

[14] *What good is it, my brothers, if a man claims to have faith but has no deeds? Can such faith save him?* [15] *Suppose a brother or sister is without clothes and daily food.* [16] *If one of you says to him, "Go, I wish you well; keep warm and well fed," but does nothing about his physical needs, what good is it?* [17] *In the same way, faith by itself, if it is not accompanied by action, is dead.*

[18] *But someone will say, "You have faith; I have deeds."*

Show me your faith without deeds, and I will show you my faith by what I do. [19] *You believe that there is one God. Good! Even the demons believe that—and shudder.*

[20] *You foolish man, do you want evidence that faith without deeds is useless[a]?* [21] *Was not our ancestor Abraham considered righteous for what he did when he offered his son Isaac on the altar?* [22] *You see that his faith and his actions were working together, and his faith was made complete by what he did.* [23] *And the scripture was fulfilled that says, "Abraham believed God, and it was credited to him as righteousness,"[b] and he was called God's friend.* [24] *You see that a person is justified by what he does and not by faith alone.*

[25] *In the same way, was not even Rahab the prostitute considered righteous for what she did when she gave lodging to the spies and sent them off in a different direction?* [26] *As the body without the spirit is dead, so faith without deeds is dead.*

[a]20 Some early manuscripts *dead*   [b]23 Gen. 15:6

READ
First Reading / First Impressions: What do you think James is concerned about?

Second Reading / Big Idea: What's the main point or topic of this passage?

SEARCH
1. What kind of "faith" is it that James condemns in verse 14 (see notes)?

2. How does the hypothetical illustration prove his point (vv. 15–16)?

3. How does he summarize his argument (v. 17; see notes)?

4. What is the objection that is lodged in response (v. 18)?

Leadership Training Supplement

YOU ARE HERE

BIRTH GROWTH RELEASE

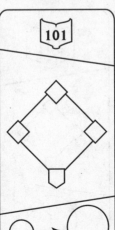

101

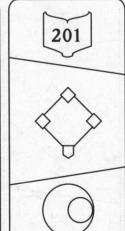

201

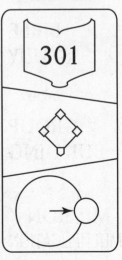

301

What is the game plan for your group in the 301 stage?

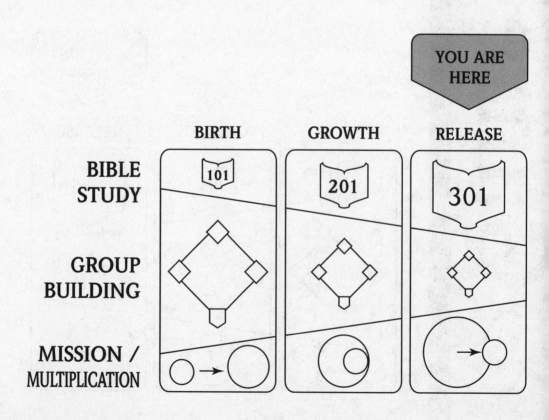

YOU ARE HERE

	BIRTH	GROWTH	RELEASE
BIBLE STUDY	101	201	301
GROUP BUILDING			
MISSION / MULTIPLICATION			

he 3-Legged Stool

The three essentials in a healthy small group are Bible Study, Group Building, and Mission / Multiplication. You need all three to stay balanced—like a 3-legged stool.

- To focus only on Bible Study will lead to scholasticism.
- To focus only on Group Building will lead to narcissism.
- To focus only on Mission will lead to burnout.

You need a game plan for the life cycle of the group where all of these elements are present in a purpose-driven strategy.

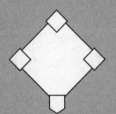

Bible Study

To develop the habit and skills for personal Bible Study.

TWO LEVELS: (1) Personal—on your own, and (2) Group study with your small group. In the personal Bible Study, you will be introduced to skills for reflection, self-inventory, creative writing and journaling.

Group Building

To move into discipleship with group accountability, shared leadership and depth community.

At the close of this course, the group building aspect will reach its goal with a "going-away" party. If there are other groups in the church in this program, the event would be for all groups. Otherwise, the group will have its own closing celebration and commissioning time.

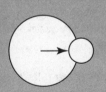

Mission / Multiplication

To commission the members of the leadership team from your group who are going to start a new group.

This Leadership Training Supplement is about your mission project. In six steps, your group will be led through a decision-making process to discover the leadership team within your group to form a new group.

Mission / Multiplication

Where are you in the 3-stage life cycle of your mission?

You can't sit on a one-legged stool—or even a two-legged stool. It takes all three. A Bible Study and Care Group that doesn't have a MISSION will fall.

Birthing Cycle

The mission is to give birth to a new group at the conclusion of this course. In this 301 course, you are supposed to be at stage three. If you are not at stage three, you can still reach the mission goal if you stay focused.

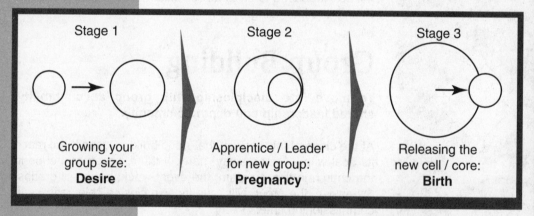

Stage 1	Stage 2	Stage 3
Growing your group size: **Desire**	Apprentice / Leader for new group: **Pregnancy**	Releasing the new cell / core: **Birth**

The birthing process begins with DESIRE. If you do not want to birth a new group, it will never happen. Desire keeps the group focused on inviting new people into your group every week—until your group grows to about 10 or 12 people.

The second stage is PREGNANCY. By recognizing the gifts of people in your group, you are able to designate two or three people who will ultimately be the missionaries in your group to form a new group. This is called the "leadership core."

The third stage is BIRTH—which takes place at the end of this course, when the whole group commissions the core or cell to move out and start the new group.

6 Steps to Birth a Group

Step 1 ## Desire

Is your group purpose-driven about mission?

Take this pop quiz and see how purpose-driven you are. Then, study the "four fallacies" about groups.

Step 2 ## Assessment

Is your church purpose-driven about groups?

Pinpoint where you are coming from and where most of the people in small groups in your church come from.

Step 3 ## Survey

Where's the itch for those in your church who are not involved in groups?

Take this churchwide survey to discover the felt needs of those in your church who do not seem to be interested in small groups.

Step 4 ## Brainstorming

What did you learn about your church from the survey?

Debrief the survey in the previous step to decide how your small group could make a difference in starting a new group.

Step 5 ## Barnstorming

Who are you going to invite?

Build a prospect list of people you think might be interested in joining a new group.

Step 6 ## Commissioning

Congratulations. You deserve a party.

Commission the leadership core from your group who are going to be your missionaries to start a new group. Then, for the rest of the "mother group," work on your covenant for starting over ... with a few empty chairs.

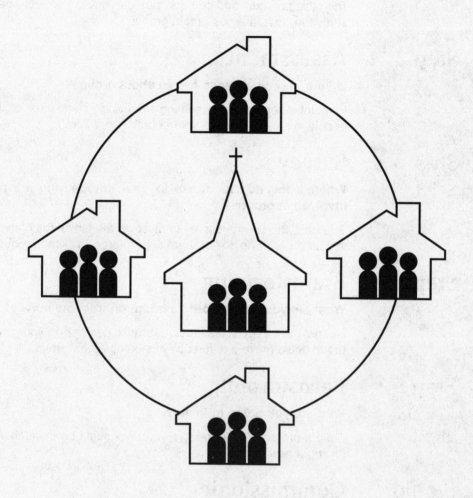

Desire

Is your group purpose-driven about mission?

The greatest danger to any chain is its strongest link. This is especially true of Bible Study groups. The very depth of the study keeps new people from joining, or feeling comfortable when they join. In the end the group grows inward, becoming self-centered and spiritually insensitive.

To prevent this from happening in your group, take this pop quiz and share the results with your group.

	Yes	No
1. Are you a committed follower of Jesus Christ?	☐	☐
2. Do you believe that Jesus Christ wants you to share your faith with others?	☐	☐
3. Do you believe that every Christian needs to belong to a small, caring community where Jesus Christ is affirmed?	☐	☐
4. Do you know of people in your church who are not presently involved in a small group?	☐	☐
5. Do you know friends on the fringe of the church who need to belong to a life-sharing small group?	☐	☐
6. Do you believe that God has a will and plan for your life?	☐	☐
7. Are you willing to be open to what God might do through you in this small group?	☐	☐
8. Are you open to the possibility that God might use you to form a new group?	☐	☐

If you can't say "No" to any of these questions, consider yourself committed!

What Is a Small Group?

A Small Group is an intentional, face-to-face gathering of people in a similar stage of life at a regular time with a common purpose of discovering and growing in a relationship with Jesus Christ.

Small Groups are the disciple-making strategy of Flamingo Road Church. The behaviors of the 12 step strategy are the goals we want to achieve with each individual in small group. These goals are accomplished through a new members class (membership) and continues in a regular on-going small group (maturity, ministry and multiplication).

Keys to an Effective Small Group Ministry

1. Care for all people (members/guests) through organized active Care Groups.
2. Teach the Bible interactively while making life application.
3. Build a Servant Leadership Team.
4. Birth New Groups.

Commitments of all Small Group Leaders are ...

... all the behaviors represented in the 12 step strategy
... to lead their group to be an effective small group as mentioned above.
... use curriculum approved by small group pastor

Taken from the Small Group Training Manual of Flamingo Road Community Church, Fort Lauderdale, FL.

Four Fallacies About Small Groups

Are you suffering from one of these four misconceptions when it comes to small groups? Check yourself on these fallacies.

Fallacy #1: It takes 10 to 12 people to start a small group.

Wrong. The best size to start with is three or four people—which leaves room in the group for growth. Start "small" and pray that God will fill the "empty chair" ... and watch it happen.

Fallacy #2: It takes a lot of skill to lead a small group.

Wrong again. Sticking to the three-part tight agenda makes it possible for nearly anyone to lead a group. For certain support and recovery groups more skills are required, but the typical Bible Study and Care Group can be led by anyone with lots of heart and vision.

Fallacy #3: To assure confidentiality, the "door" should be closed after the first session.

For certain "high risk" groups this is true; but for the average Bible Study and Care Group all you need is the rule that "nothing that is said in the group is discussed outside of the group."

Fallacy #4: The longer the group lasts, the better it gets.

Not necessarily. The bell curve for effective small groups usually peaks in the second year. Unless new life is brought into the group, the group will decline in vitality. It is better to release the group (and become a reunion group) when it is at its peak than to run the risk of burnout.

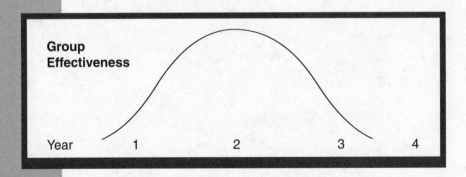

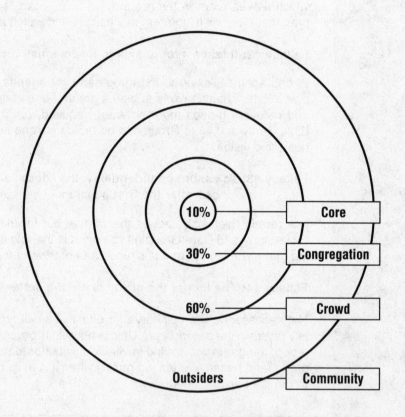

Step 2

Assessment

Is your church purpose-driven about groups?

Most of the people who come to small groups in the church are from the highly committed CORE of the church. How about your group?

Pinpoint Your Group

The graph on the opposite page represents the four types of people typically found in your church and in your community.

- **10% Core:** The "spiritual core" of the church and the church leadership.

- **30% Congregation:** Those who come to church regularly and are faithful in giving.

- **60% Crowd:** Those on the membership roles who attend only twice a year. They have fallen through the cracks.

- **Outside Community:** Those who live in the surrounding area but do not belong to any church.

Step 1: On the opposite page, put a series of dots in the appropriate circles where the members of your group come from.

Step 2: If you know of other small groups in your church, put some more dots on the graph to represent the people in those groups. When you are finished, stop and ask your group this question:

"Why do the groups in our church appeal only to the people who are represented by the dots on this graph?"

Four Kinds of Small Groups

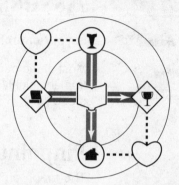

SUPPORT / RECOVERY GROUPS

- Felt needs
- Short-term
- Low-level commitment
- Seeker Bible Study

These groups are designed to appeal to hurting people on the fringe of the church and in the community.

PULPIT-BASED GROUPS

- Around the Scripture in the Sunday lesson
- With handout in Sunday bulletin
- With discussion questions
- No homework

These groups are designed to appeal to those who come to church and listen to the sermon but do not want to do homework.

DISCIPLESHIP / DEPTH BIBLE STUDY GROUPS

- Year-long commitment
- Depth Bible Study
- Homework required
- Curriculum based

These groups are designed to appeal to the 10% highly committed core of the church who are ready for discipleship.

COVENANT GROUPS

- Three-stage life cycle
- Renewal option
- Begins with 7-week contract
- Graded levels of Bible Study: 101, 201 and 301

Church Evaluation

You do NOT have to complete this assessment if you are not in the leadership core of your church, but it would be extremely valuable if your group does have members in the leadership core of your church.

1. Currently, what percentage of your church members are involved in small groups?

2. What kind of small groups are you offering in your church? (Study the four kinds of groups on the opposite page.)
   ❑ Support / Recovery Groups
   ❑ Pulpit-Based Groups
   ❑ Discipleship / Depth Bible Study Groups
   ❑ Three-stage Covenant Groups

3. Which statement below represents the position of your church on small groups?
   ❑ "Small Groups have never been on the drawing board at our church."
   ❑ "We have had small groups, but they fizzled."
   ❑ "Our church leadership has had negative experiences with small groups."
   ❑ "Small groups are the hope for our future."
   ❑ "We have Sunday school; that's plenty."

4. How would you describe the people who usually get involved in small groups?
   ❑ 10% Core   ❑ 30% Congregation   ❑ 60% Crowd

Risk and Supervision
This depends on the risk level of the group—the higher the risk, the higher the supervision. For the typical Bible Study group ⬲, pulpit-based group ⓨ, or covenant group ◈ (where there is little risk), supervision is minimal. For some support groups ♡ and all recovery groups ⓥ, training and supervision are required.

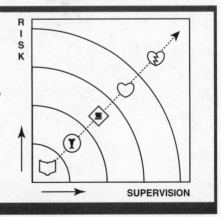

Step 3

Survey

Where's the itch for those in your church who are not involved in groups?

This survey has been written for churchwide use—in hopes that you may be able to rewrite it and use it in your own church. The courses described in this survey are taken from the present Serendipity 101, 201 and 301 courses for small groups.

Churchwide Survey for Small Groups

Name_____Phone_____

Section 1: Interest in Shared-Experience Groups

A shared-experience group is short-term in nature (7–13 weeks) and brings people together based on a common interest, experience or need in their lives. The various topics being considered for shared-experience groups are listed below.

1. Which of these shared-experience courses might be of interest to you? Check all that apply in the grid below under question 1 (**Q1**).

2. Which of these shared-experience groups would you be interested in hosting or co-leading? Check all that apply in the grid below under question 2 (**Q2**).

3. Which of these shared-experience groups do you think would be of interest to a friend or relative of yours who is on the fringe of the church? Check all that apply in the grid below under question 3 (**Q3**).

[101] VIDEO Electives — 7–13 weeks: Sunday School with Groups

	Q1	Q2	Q3
1. Dealing With Grief & Loss (Hope in the Midst of Pain)	☐	☐	☐
2. Divorce Recovery (Picking Up the Pieces)	☐	☐	☐
3. Marriage Enrichment (Making a Good Marriage Better)	☐	☐	☐
4. Parenting Adolescents (Easing the Way to Adulthood)	☐	☐	☐
5. Healthy Relationships (Living Within Defined Boundaries)	☐	☐	☐
6. Stress Management (Finding the Balance)	☐	☐	☐
7. 12 Steps (The Path to Wholeness)	☐	☐	☐

Survey The Needs —

101 **BEGINNER Bible Study — 7- to 13-week groups**

	Q1	Q2	Q3
8. Stressed Out (Keeping Your Cool)	☐	☐	☐
9. Core Values (Setting My Moral Compass)	☐	☐	☐
10. Marriage (Seasons of Growth)	☐	☐	☐
11. Jesus (Up Close & Personal)	☐	☐	☐
12. Gifts & Calling (Discovering God's Will)	☐	☐	☐
13. Relationships (Learning to Love)	☐	☐	☐
14. Assessment (Personal Audit)	☐	☐	☐
15. Family (Stages of Parenting)	☐	☐	☐
16. Wholeness (Time for a Checkup)	☐	☐	☐
17. Beliefs (Basic Christianity)	☐	☐	☐

201 **DEEPER Bible Study — Varying Length Courses**

	Q1	Q2	Q3
18. Supernatural: Amazing Stories (Jesus' Miracles) 13 wks.	☐	☐	☐
19. Discipleship: In His Steps (Life of Christ) 13 wks.	☐	☐	☐
20. Wisdom: The Jesus Classics (Jesus' Parables) 13 wks.	☐	☐	☐
21. Challenge: Attitude Adjustment (Sermon on the Mount) 13 wks.	☐	☐	☐
22. Endurance: Running the Race (Philippians) 11 wks.	☐	☐	☐
23. Teamwork: Together in Christ (Ephesians) 12 wks.	☐	☐	☐
24. Integrity: Taking on Tough Issues (1 Corinthians) 12–23 wks.		☐	☐
25. Gospel: Jesus of Nazareth (Gospel of Mark) 13–26 wks.	☐	☐	☐
26. Leadership: Passing the Torch (1 & 2 Timothy) 14 wks.	☐	☐	☐
27. Excellence: Mastering the Basics (Romans) 15–27 wks.	☐	☐	☐
28. Hope: Looking at the End of Time (Revelation) 13–26 wks.	☐	☐	☐
29. Faithfulness: Walking in the Light (1 John) 11 wks.	☐	☐	☐
30. Freedom: Living by Grace (Galatians) 13 wks.	☐	☐	☐
31. Perseverance: Staying the Course (1 Peter) 10 wks.	☐	☐	☐
32. Performance: Faith at Work (James) 12 wks.	☐	☐	☐

301 **DEPTH Bible Study — 13-week groups**

	Q1	Q2	Q3
33. Ephesians (Our Riches in Christ)	☐	☐	☐
34. James (Walking the Talk)	☐	☐	☐
35. Life of Christ (Behold the Man)	☐	☐	☐
36. Miracles (Signs and Wonders)	☐	☐	☐
37. Parables (Virtual Reality)	☐	☐	☐
38. Philippians (Joy Under Stress)	☐	☐	☐
39. Sermon on the Mount (Examining Your Life)	☐	☐	☐
40. 1 John (The Test of Faith)	☐	☐	☐

Section 2: Covenant Groups (Long-term)

A covenant group is longer term (like an extended family), starting with a commitment for 7–13 weeks, with an option of renewing your covenant for the rest of the year. A covenant group can decide to change the topics they study over time. The general themes for the covenant groups that our church is considering are listed on the previous two pages.

4. Which of the following long-term covenant groups would you be interested in?

❐ Singles	❐ Men	❐ Women
❐ Couples	❐ Parents	❐ Downtown
❐ Twenty-Something	❐ Thirty-Something	❐ Empty Nesters
❐ Mixed	❐ Breakfast	❐ Engineers
❐ Young Marrieds	❐ Seniors	❐ Sunday Brunch

Section 3: Pre-Covenant Groups (Short-term)

To give you a taste of a small group, our church is offering a 7-week "trial" program for groups. For this trial program, the group will use the course *Beginnings: A Taste of Serendipity.*

5. Would you be interested in joining a "trial" group?

❐ Yes   ❐ No   ❐ Maybe

6. What would be the most convenient time and place for you to meet?

❐ Weekday morning   ❐ At church
❐ Weekday evening   ❐ In a home
❐ Saturday morning
❐ Sunday after church

7. What kind of group would you prefer?

❐ Men
❐ Women
❐ Singles
❐ Couples
❐ Mixed
❐ Parents
❐ Seniors
❐ Around my age
❐ Doesn't matter

SERENDIPITY

BEGINNINGS
A TASTE OF SERENDIPITY

7 Sessions To Become
A Great Small Group!

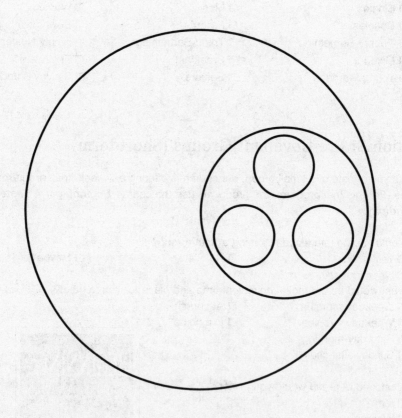

Step 4 Brainstorming

What did you learn about your church from the survey?

The Itch: Debrief together what you discovered from the survey about the need for small groups in your church. To begin with, find out in your group who checked Q3 for any of the 101 Video and 101 Beginner Electives (courses 1–17). Jot down in the box below the top three courses that you checked for 1–17.

Top Three Courses:

The Nitch: For the top three courses in the box above, find out if anyone in your group checked Q2 for these courses—i.e., that they would be willing to host or help lead a group that was interested in this course. Jot down the names of those in your group who checked Q2 in the box below.

Potential Hosts and Leaders:

The Apprentice / Leader and Leadership Core: Now, as a group, look over the names of the potential hosts and leaders you put in the box above and try to discern the person on this list who you think could easily be the leader of this new group, and one or two others who might fill out the Leadership Core for this new group. Jot down these names in the box below.

Apprentice / Leader and Leadership Core:

Q&A

What is the purpose of Covenant Groups?*

The members of the Covenant Group come together for the purpose of helping each other to:

- *Love God with all their heart, soul, mind and strength (Mark 12:30).*
- *Love their neighbors as themselves (Mark 12:31).*
- *Make disciples (Matthew 28:19).*

What are the qualifications of a Covenant Group leader?

A Covenant Group leader functions as a lay pastor, taking on himself or herself the responsibility of providing the primary care for the members of the group. Therefore, a Covenant Group leader exemplifies the following characteristics:

- *believes in Jesus Christ as their Lord and Savior*
- *has been a Christian for a while*
- *continues to grow in their faith*
- *cares for the well-being of others*
- *is able to set goals and work toward them*
- *demonstrates moral integrity*
- *listens to others*
- *is empathetic*
- *is willing to learn from others*
- *demonstrates flexibility*
- *respects others*
- *senses a call to serve*

A Covenant Group leader is not a perfect person! He or she need not know everything about leading and caring for others. Skills valuable to the role of a leader will be taught throughout the year, and care for the leader will be provided on an ongoing basis through a coach.

A Covenant Group leader is not necessarily a teacher. It is far more important that the leader be able to shepherd and care for the others in the group. Teaching is often a shared responsibility among group members.

* These four pages (M20–M23) are taken from the Training Manual For Group Leaders at Zionsville Presbyterian Church, Zionsville, IN, and are used by permission.

What does the church expect of a Covenant Group leader?

Every leader is asked to agree to the terms of the leader's covenant. Covenant Group leaders are to attend the monthly STP (Sharing, Training and Prayer) meeting. This gathering is held for the purposes of training and supporting leaders. The meeting takes place on the third Tuesday of each month, from 6:45 p.m. to 8:30 p.m. The two main elements of the STP event concern communication. The first half of the evening is devoted to disseminating the vision. The second half of the meeting consists of leaders huddling with their coach and with each other for the purpose of learning from one another. If a leader is unable to attend this meeting for some significant reason, he or she is to arrange another time to meet with their coach.

Leaders are also to fill out the Group Leader's Summary after every group event. This one-page reporting form takes only 10 minutes or so to complete and is a vital communication link between the staff liaison, the coach and the leader.

What can a Covenant Group leader expect in the way of support from the church?

A Covenant Group leader can expect the session and the staff to hold to the terms laid out in the Church's Covenant.

Every leader will be given a coach. This coach is someone whose ministry is to care for up to five leaders. The coach is charged with the responsibility of resourcing, encouraging, supporting, evaluating, challenging, loving and listening to the leaders in his or her care.

Every coach is supported by a staff member. If leaders ever have a situation where they feel that their coach is unable to help them, the staff liaison is there to be of assistance.

What is the role of a Covenant Group leader?

When people come together in groups, the group itself becomes an entity that is greater than the sum of its parts. The Covenant Group leader watches over the life and health of this new entity.

Specifically the Covenant Group leader is to:

- *find an apprentice*
- *pray and prepare for group meetings*
- *notify their coach or staff of acute crisis conditions requiring response*
- *develop and maintain an atmosphere in which members of the group can discover and develop God-given spiritual gifts*
- *pray for the spiritual growth and protection of each member*
- *refer counseling cases that exceed experience level*
- *convene the group two to four times each month*
- *recruit a host/hostess, when appropriate, and to see that child care and refreshments are available and a venue is arranged*
- *develop a healthy balance of love, learn, do, decide*
- *assure God's redemptive agenda via Scripture, sharing, prayers, songs and worship*
- *assist the group in refraining from divisiveness or teachings contrary to church position*
- *accept responsibility for group growth through the open-chair strategy*
- *lead an exemplary life*
- *regularly touch base with members outside the context of the group meeting just to say "Hi" and to see how they are doing*
- *help the group form a covenant and to review the covenant periodically*

While the Covenant Group leader takes primary responsibility for these activities, he or she should involve members of the group in many of them.

Does a Covenant Group really have to have a leader?

Yes! Without a leader a Covenant Group is like a ship at sea with no captain. A ship without a captain is at the mercy of the prevailing current and is unable to prepare for what may lie ahead. However, a ship with a captain has her course mapped out, and there is always someone at the helm ready to respond if necessary. So it is with a Covenant Group. The leader serves the others in the group by working to chart the best course as they together pursue being God's people on earth.

What are the critical elements of a Covenant Group?

A Covenant Group needs to have:

- *a leader*
- *an apprentice / leader*
- *members*
- *an open chair*
- *a covenant (see page M32)*

What is an Apprentice / Leader and how do we find one?

An apprentice / leader is someone who agrees that in time he or she will step out into leadership. Historically churches have tended to ask only those who aggressively step forward to serve in leadership positions. Rarely have churches worked at developing leaders. The result has been that most churches experience the phenomenon where only 20% of the congregation does 80% of the work. This historical approach stifles the giftedness of 80% of the church's population! In addition, the church has burned out many of their stand-out leaders by asking them to lead too many programs and too many people. Without some form of apprentice / leadership development, the church is constrained to overload its highly motivated, "here-I-am-send-me" leaders. The apprentice / leader model is meant to address these concerns.

The apprentice / leader is not an assistant. An assistant seldom has plans of stepping into the leader's shoes. Instead, the apprentice / leader works alongside the leader, with the intent of one day becoming a leader themselves. Along the way he or she is experiencing on-the-job training, learning the skills necessary to serve a small group as its leader.

It is the responsibility of the leader to find an apprentice / leader. The most important tools for the leader in this process are prayer and observation. The leader should pray, asking God to send someone whom he or she could mentor and train as a leader. Accompanying these prayers should be efforts to observe those who demonstrate signs of giftedness in shepherding, organizing, listening and faith. The one who is on time and who routinely prepares diligently for the group could be a candidate. The leader could also begin using the time before and after worship services, as well as various fellowship and educational events, to meet others in the congregation. As relationships are established, and the extent of a leader's acquaintances are broadened, the opportunity for finding a suitable apprentice / leader increases.

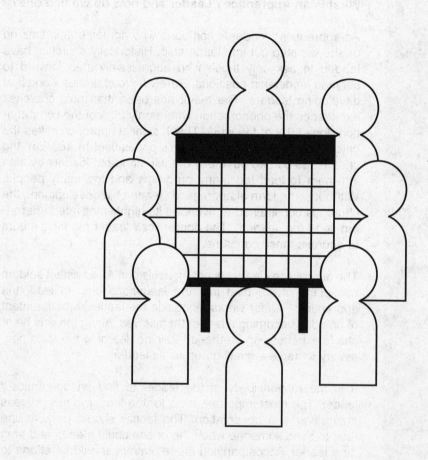

Step 5

Barnstorming

Who are you going to invite?

In the previous step, you identified the Apprentice / Leader and one or two others in your group who are going to be the leadership cell or core to start a new group.

Now, as a whole group, spend a few minutes creating a prospect list of people you would like to invite into this new group. Ask someone in your group to be the secretary and write down in the boxes below the names of people who come to mind:

Friends: Who are your friends in the church who you think might be interested in a small group?

Affinity: What are the special interests of the people in your leadership cell and who are the people in your church with the same interests? For instance, if the people in your leadership cell love tennis, who are the people in your church who might be interested in a small group before tennis? What about book lovers, entrepreneurs, empty nesters, senior citizens, stock watchers, etc.?

How Serendipity 101 Courses
Make Leading A Beginner Group Easy:

1. Each session has get acquainted **Ice-Breakers** to get your group started and a **3-Part Tight Agenda** to keep it on track!

2. Two Options for breaking open the Word:
- **Option1: Light**—for people who are not familiar with the Bible
- **Option 2: Heavy**—for people who are familiar with the Bible

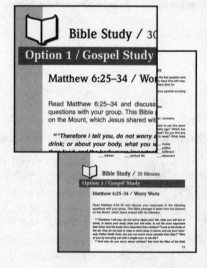

3. Study Helps for the Group Leader include Margin Tips, Reference Notes and Guided Questionnaires for Bible Study.

Who Do We Invite?

Felt Needs: Who are the people you know with the same felt needs? These people might be on the fringe of the church or even outside of the church. Go back to the survey on pages M15–M16 (the 101 courses) and think of people you feel could be hot prospects. For instance, who would be interested in "Stressed Out," "Marriage," "Wholeness," "Healthy Relationships," "Parenting Adolescents," etc.?

Geographical Location: Where do the people in your leadership team live or work, and who are the people in your church in the same area?

The Four Circles: Now, on this diagram, pinpoint the people you have jotted down in the four circles. Do you have any people on this list from the **Crowd** (the church dropouts)? Do you have anyone on your list from the **Community** (who do not attend any church)? It's really important that you have people from all four circles on your list.

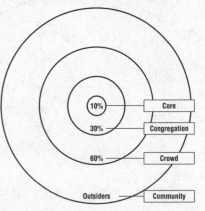

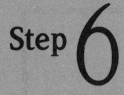

Step **6**

Commissioning

Congratulations. You deserve a party.

Only two things remain for you to decide: (1) How are you going to commission the leadership team for the new group and (2) What is the rest of your group going to do next?

Going-away party

You have several options. If the church is planning a church-wide event for all of the groups (such as a graduation banquet), you would have a table at this event for your group. If your church is not planning an event, you must plan your own going-away party.

At this party, you may want to reminisce about your life together as a group with the questions below, have fun making some "Wild Predictions" (see page M30), share a Bible Study time (see page M31), and conclude with a time of commissioning and prayer.

Reminiscing Questions

1. What do you remember about the first time you attended this group?

2. How did you feel about opening up in this group and sharing your story?

3. What was the funniest thing that happened in this group?

4. What was the high point for you in this group?

5. What will you miss most about this group?

6. How would you like this group to stay in touch with each other after you multiply?

7. How did this group contribute to your life?

8. What is the biggest change that has occurred in your life since joining this group?

Leadership Training

Wild Predictions

Try to match the people in your group to the crazy forecasts below. (Don't take it too seriously; it's meant to be fun!) Read out loud the first item and ask everyone to call out the name of the person who is most likely to accomplish this feat. Then, read the next item and ask everyone to make a new prediction, etc.

THE PERSON IN OUR GROUP MOST LIKELY TO ...

Make a million selling Beanie Babies over the Internet

Become famous for designing new attire for sumo wrestlers

Replace Vanna White on *Wheel of Fortune*

Appear on *The Tonight Show* to exhibit an acrobatic talent

Move to a desert island

Discover a new use for underarm deodorant

Succeed David Letterman as host of *The Late Show*

Substitute for John Madden as Fox's football color analyst

Appear on the cover of *Muscle & Fitness Magazine*

Become the newest member of the Spice Girls

Work as a bodyguard for Rush Limbaugh at Feminist convention

Write a best-selling novel based on their love life

Be a dance instructor on a cruise ship for wealthy, well-endowed widows

Win the blue ribbon at the state fair for best Rocky Mountain oyster recipe

Land a job as head librarian for Amazon.com

Be the first woman to win the Indianapolis 500

Open the Clouseau Private Detective Agency

Going-Away Party

Reflection Bible Study

Barnabas and Saul Sent Off — Acts 13:1–3, NIV

13 In the church at Antioch there were prophets and teachers: Barnabas, Simeon called Niger, Lucius of Cyrene, Manaen (who had been brought up with Herod the tetrarch) and Saul. ²While they were worshiping the Lord and fasting, the Holy Spirit said, "Set apart for me Barnabas and Saul for the work to which I have called them." ³So after they had fasted and prayed, they placed their hands on them and sent them off.

1. Why do you think God chose this small group in Antioch to launch the first missionary journey (instead of the church headquarters in Jerusalem)?
   - ❑ It was merely coincidental.
   - ❑ They were following the leading of the Holy Spirit.
   - ❑ They were a bunch of outcasts from the fringe of the church.
   - ❑ They didn't know how to "paint inside the lines."

2. How do you think the leadership back in Jerusalem felt when they heard what these guys were doing?
   - ❑ thrilled
   - ❑ embarrassed
   - ❑ angry that they didn't follow protocol
   - ❑ They probably didn't hear about it until later.

3. Why do you think the small group chose two people to send out instead of one?
   - ❑ for companionship
   - ❑ They had different gifts: Paul was a hothead, Barnabas an encourager.
   - ❑ It was coincidental.

4. As you think about sending out some members of your small group to give "birth" to a new group, what is your greatest concern for these people?
   - ❑ keeping the faith
   - ❑ keeping the vision
   - ❑ keeping their personal walk with Christ
   - ❑ keeping in touch with us for support

5. As one who is going to lead or colead a new group, how would you describe your emotions right now?
   - ❑ a nervous wreck
   - ❑ pregnant with excitement
   - ❑ delivery room jitters
   - ❑ Ask me next week.

6. If you could say one word of encouragement to those who are going to be new leaders, what would it be?
   - ❑ I'll be praying for you.
   - ❑ Call me anytime.
   - ❑ You can do it.
   - ❑ It's okay to fail.

What do we do next?

For those who are going to stay with the "mother group," you need to decide on your new covenant and who you are going to invite to fill the empty chairs left by the departing "missionaries."

Do we ever meet again?

Definitely! Plan NOW for "homecoming" next year when the new group returns for a time of celebration. Four good times: the World Series, Super Bowl, Final Four and Stanley Cup.

Group Covenant

Any group can benefit from creating or renewing a group covenant. Take some time for those remaining in the "mother group" to discuss the following questions. When everyone in the group has the same expectations for the group, everything runs more smoothly.

1. The purpose of our group is:

2. The goals of our group are:

3. We will meet for _____ weeks, after which we will decide if we wish to continue as a group. If we do decide to continue, we will reconsider this covenant.

4. We will meet _____ (weekly, every other week, monthly).

5. Our meetings will be from _____ o'clock to _____ o'clock, and we will strive to start and end on time.

6. We will meet at _____ or rotate from house to house.

7. We will take care of the following details: ❏ child care ❏ refreshments

8. We agree to the following rules for our group:

   ❏ PRIORITY: While we are in this group, group meetings have priority.

   ❏ PARTICIPATION: Everyone is given the right to their own opinion and all questions are respected.

   ❏ CONFIDENTIALITY: Anything said in the meeting is not to be repeated outside the meeting.

   ❏ EMPTY CHAIR: The group stays open to new people and invites prospective members to visit the group.

   ❏ SUPPORT: Permission is given to call each other in times of need.

   ❏ ADVICE GIVING: Unsolicited advice is not allowed.

   ❏ MISSION: We will do everything in our power to start a new group.

5. What is James' answer (v. 18; see notes)?

6. What is the lesson in Abraham's experience (vv. 22–23)?

7. What is the point (v. 24; see note)?

8. What is the lesson in Rahab's experience (v. 25)?

9. What is the point (v. 26)?

APPLY

Imagine that the government suddenly outlawed Christianity. If you were arrested for being a Christian, what evidence could be brought against you? Answer this question in the third person, as would be found in a police investigative report. For example—"The following evidence was found against Joan: She ..."

GROUP AGENDA

After the first part, read the Scripture out loud and divide into groups of 4. Then come back together for the third part.

TO BEGIN / 10–15 Min. (Choose 1 or 2)

1. Are you a doer or a thinker? Are you more likely to act without thinking, or think without acting?

2. Who is one person you admire for how their lifestyle grows out of their beliefs?

3. When helping those in need, do you more often give your time, money or services?

TO GO DEEPER / 30 Min. (Choose 2 or 3)

1. If you did the homework, choose one question in READ or SEARCH and give your answer—or share about a question or issue you struggled with.

2. What is the difference between "faith" as James uses it here and the way "faith" is normally defined in the New Testament?

3. Which comes first—faith or action?

4. If James were living today, how strongly do you think he would make the point of this passage?

5. Have you ever been challenged to put your faith to the test in a critical way, like Abraham was?

6. CASE STUDY: Bob gave up his lucrative medical practice in the suburbs and moved into the city, where he gives his time to a poor neighborhood clinic. His friends think he is crazy. Even the friends in his church think he is crazy. What do you think?

TO CLOSE / 15–30 Min.

1. Are you thinking and dreaming about your group's mission? (See the center section.)

2. What did you write for the "police report" in APPLY?

3. By the definition of "faith" in this passage, would you say that your faith is alive, dead, snoozing or just waking up?

4. How would you like the group to pray for you this week?

NOTES

Summary. This is part two of James' discussion of the poor. In part one (2:1–13) the issue was discrimination against the poor. Here the issue is charity toward the poor. This section parallels the previous section structurally. Both sections begin with a key assertion which is then illustrated. This is followed by a logical argument which demonstrates the point. The section is then concluded with two arguments drawn from the Bible. This discussion of charity toward the poor is set in the larger context of the relationship between faith and works. At first glance, it would appear that James is saying exactly the opposite of what Paul taught (see, for example, Rom. 3:28 and Gal. 2:16). In fact, the difference is more apparent than real. The key issue for Paul is how one gains right-standing before God, while for James the issue is how one demonstrates to others the claim to have such right-standing. Paul's focus is inward. It centers on a person's relationship to God. In contrast, James' focus is outward. It centers on relationships with other people. Paul writes about how one *begins* the Christian life, while James writes about how one *lives* the Christian life. The issue for Paul is *justification,* while the issue for James is *sanctification.* Both would agree that men and women are saved by Christ through faith for works.

2:14 my brothers. By this phrase James signals the start of a new point.

faith. James uses this word in a special way. The faith he speaks of here is mere intellectual affirmation. Such a mind-oriented profession stands in sharp contrast to the comprehensive, whole-life commitment that characterizes true New Testament faith. New Testament faith involves believing with all one's being: mind, emotions, body (behavior) and spirit. The people James has in mind differ from their pagan and Jewish neighbors only in what they profess to believe. They are orthodox Christians who believe in Jesus—however, they live no differently than anyone else.

deeds. Just as James uses the word "faith" in his own way, so too he uses "deeds" (or "works"). For James, deeds have to do with proper ethical behavior. In contrast, Paul seldom calls such behavior "works." In fact, he generally avoids the word altogether and when he does use it, he equates it to the Law, i.e., "works of the Law" which clearly is not what the Christian life is all about.

Can such faith save him? The implied answer to this rhetorical question is "No." This answer is based on what James just said in 2:12–13. Intellectual faith cannot save one from judgment when one has not been merciful (see also Matt. 25:31–46 and 1 John 3:17–18).

2:15 Suppose. A test case is proposed through which the absurdity of claiming "faith" without corresponding "action" is made evident. Though this is a hypothetical situation, it would not have been uncommon in Jerusalem for a person to lack the basics of life given the famine and the marginal economy of the area.

a brother or sister. James picks an example in which the right action is absolutely clear. The person in need is a Christian from their own fellowship, not an outsider or a person far away about whom their responsibility might not be as unequivocal.

clothes and daily food. Both are absolutely necessary to sustain life. A person without food and without warmth will die. The reference to clothes can be either to the outer tunic which was worn in public and which served as a blanket, or it can refer to clothes so ragged that they are of little use. This word can also be translated as "naked," having no clothes at all (as in Mark 14:51–52).

2:16 The implication is that the Christian to whom this appeal has been made could meet the need but chooses not to and instead offers pious platitudes.

2:17 James did not dream up his conclusion here. It is what is taught consistently throughout the New Testament. John the Baptist taught it (Luke 3:8). Jesus taught it (Matt. 5:16; 7:15–21). And Paul taught it (Rom. 2:6; 14:12; 1 Cor. 3:8; 2 Cor. 5:10).

dead. James is saying, "Your faith is not real, it is a sham, it is make believe, it is nominal. You are playing at being a Christian."

2:18 Show me your faith without deeds. Here James replies to the imaginary critic who says, "You have faith; I have deeds." James argues that faith is invisible without deeds. If faith does not make itself known in one's lifestyle, then it is nonexistent. Deeds are the only demonstration of inner faith. James disagrees that faith and deeds are unconnected. It is not a matter of either/or. It is both/and, as he shows in verse 22.

2:19 James continues to press his argument. These people say they believe so he begins with the *Shema*, the central belief of both Jew and Christian: "Hear, O Israel: The Lord our God, the Lord is one"

(see Deut. 6:4–5 and Mark 12:28–34). But then he goes on to point out that even the demons believe this (see Mark 1:23–24; 5:1–7 and Acts 16:16–18). And they respond with a shudder because they know that God is more powerful than they and that they are in rebellion against God. Belief in one God does not automatically lead to godly action. Orthodox faith alone—which the demons have—is not enough without an obedient lifestyle.

2:20 You foolish man. The NIV blunts the harshness of James' language here. "You fool," he is saying. "You empty man" is the literal rendering of this phrase. This was not an uncommon way for first-century preachers to address their listeners, especially when they were using the so-called diatribe style of speaking or writing. Even Jesus used this sort of strong language (see Matt. 23:17).

2:21–25 James concludes by offering via two illustrations from the Old Testament the evidence demanded by the fool in verse 20 for the assertion that faith is useless without deeds. In both cases faith is demonstrated by means of concrete action. Abraham actually had the knife raised over his beloved son Isaac, and Rahab actually hid the spies. Without faith, Abraham would never have even considered sacrificing his only son, nor would Rahab have defied her king at great personal risk.

2:22 This is the heart of James' argument: faith and deeds working together characterize the life of the person who is truly religious.

made complete. The idea is not that faith is somehow perfected by deeds. Rather, faith is brought to new maturity by such actions (see 1:4).

2:24 by faith alone. For James, faith means " 'by intellectual belief that God is one' or 'that Jesus is Lord,' whereas faith for Paul means personal commitment to Christ that leads inevitably to obedience because one is convinced that Jesus is Lord. ... James' point is that God will not approve a person just because he or she is very orthodox or can pass a test in systematic theology. He will declare someone righteous only if this faith is such that the person acts on it and produces the natural result of commitment, obedient action" (Davids, GNC).

2:25 Rahab. Joshua sent two spies into Jericho. Their presence was detected but Rahab hid them, sent the king's soldiers off on a wild-goose chase, and then let the spies safely down the city wall (Josh. 2:1–21).

UNIT 7—Taming the Tongue / James 3:1–12

Taming the Tongue

3 ¹Not many of you should presume to be teachers, my brothers, because you know that we who teach will be judged more strictly. ²We all stumble in many ways. If anyone is never at fault in what he says, he is a perfect man, able to keep his whole body in check.

³When we put bits into the mouths of horses to make them obey us, we can turn the whole animal. ⁴Or take ships as an example. Although they are so large and are driven by strong winds, they are steered by a very small rudder wherever the pilot wants to go. ⁵Likewise the tongue is a small part of the body, but it makes great boasts. Consider what a great forest is set on fire by a small spark. ⁶The tongue also is a fire, a world of evil among the parts of the body. It cor- rupts the whole person, sets the whole course of his life on fire, and is itself set on fire by hell.

⁷All kinds of animals, birds, reptiles and creatures of the sea are being tamed and have been tamed by man, ⁸but no man can tame the tongue. It is a restless evil, full of deadly poison.

⁹With the tongue we praise our Lord and Father, and with it we curse men, who have been made in God's likeness. ¹⁰Out of the same mouth come praise and cursing. My brothers, this should not be. ¹¹Can both fresh water and salt*ᵃ* water flow from the same spring? ¹²My brothers, can a fig tree bear olives, or a grapevine bear figs? Neither can a salt spring produce fresh water.

ᵃ11 Greek *bitter* (see also verse 14)

READ
First Reading / First Impressions: This passage makes me feel like:

❏ I'd better shut up!

❏ Why did I speak like I did today?

❏ I wish _____ would read this.

❏ other:_____

Second Reading / Big Idea: How would you sum up James' point here in one sentence?

SEARCH
1. Why is teaching the Scripture a dangerous responsibility (v. 1; see notes)?

2. What does verse 2 teach about human behavior (v. 2; see notes)?

3. What is the point of the first two illustrations (vv. 3–4; see notes)?

4. What new element is introduced in the third illustration (vv. 5–6)?

5. What is the contrast in verses 7–8?

6. If no one can tame his/her tongue, where do you suppose we can find help (see Gal. 5:22–25)?

7. What is the point of the image in verses 9–12 (particularly in verse 10)?

APPLY

Make a study of the word "tongue" and any images that are used to characterize the tongue in this passage. In the left column, jot down the verse reference, and in the right column note what is said about the word "tongue" in this verse.

REFERENCE	POINT OR TEACHING

In what way do you need to change the way you use your tongue?

GROUP AGENDA

After the first part, read the Scripture out loud and divide into groups of 4. Then come back together for the third part.

TO BEGIN / 10–15 Min. (Choose 1 or 2)
1. Who was one of your favorite teachers in school? Why?

2. Are you more likely to blurt out your feelings or to hold them in?

3. Who gets the brunt of your sharp tongue?

TO GO DEEPER / 30 Min. (Choose 2 or 3)
1. Why is it such a great responsibility to be a teacher, especially of the Scripture?

2. Why are the illustrations of a horse's bit, a ship's rudder, and a fire's spark so fitting regarding the tongue?

3. If verse 8 is true, why should we even try to control our tongues?

4. In your everyday conversation, how seriously do you take verse 9? What does this verse say about the caution, and the reverence, with which we must choose our words?

5. Jesus and the apostles Peter and Paul were not always very "tame" when it came to the tongue. When is harsh language acceptable? Do you feel you are able to use strong language when appropriate, and refrain when appropriate?

6. CASE STUDY: Your teenager uses abusive language to ventilate feelings, especially toward your spouse. The counselor feels this is healthy. What do you think?

TO CLOSE / 15–30 Min.
1. Are you happy with your group's progress on developing your mission?

2. How did you answer the second question in APPLY?

3. What have you found helpful in controlling your tongue?

4. How can the group pray for you?

NOTES

Summary. James now shifts to his second subject: wisdom. This discussion will extend from 3:1 to 4:12. In this first section he examines the connection between speech and wisdom. In particular, he focuses on the tongue, that organ by which we produce words, the vehicles of wisdom. Words, he says, are not insignificant. Words can be wise but they can also be deadly. The tongue is such a small organ and yet it has great power. It can control the very direction of one's life. The mature person is known by his or her ability to control the tongue. It is theorized that the context for this discussion was a problem faced by the Jerusalem church. Certain teachers were using their tongues to criticize others (and were probably being criticized in return).

3:1 *Not many of you should presume to become teachers.* In the early church a person did not become a teacher by going to seminary or Bible school. None existed. Instead, teachers were called and empowered by the Holy Spirit (see Rom. 12:6–7; 1 Cor. 12:28; Eph. 4:11–13). The problem was that the gift of teaching could be faked. It was a prestigious position and if a person were eloquent, he or she might pretend to be a teacher. False teachers were a real problem in the first century (see 1 Tim. 1:7; Titus 1:11; 2 Peter 2:1–3).

teachers. Following in the tradition of the rabbis, early Christian teachers were responsible for the moral and spiritual instruction of a local congregation. This was an especially important task in the first century since many of the Christians, being poor, would not have been very well educated. Nor could they read or write. In contrast to apostles whose ministry was itinerant, teachers stayed in one location and taught a particular congregation. Teachers were held in great honor, but herein lay great danger. They might become puffed up with spiritual and intellectual pride (see Matt. 23:2–7). They might begin to teach their own opinions instead of God's truth. (The Judaizers did this when they started teaching that before people could become Christians they first had to become Jews and be circumcised—see Acts 15:1–29.) Or teachers might turn out to be hypocrites—teaching one thing but living another (see Rom. 2:17–24).

judged more strictly. It is dangerous to fake the gift of teaching (see Matt. 12:36; 23:1–33; Mark 12:40). To mislead God's people by false words or an inappropriate lifestyle can cause great harm to those seeking to know God and follow his ways.

3:2 stumble. This word means "to trip, to slip up or to make a mistake." This is not deliberate, premeditated wrong-doing. Rather, it is failure due to inadequacy. This is a problem of faulty *reactions*, not evil *actions*.

what he says. James' focus is on words, the stock-in-trade of teachers. Thus James launches into the main theme of this section: the sins of the tongue. This is a common theme in Scripture (Prov. 10:19; 15:1–4; 21:23; Eccl. 5:2–3; Matt. 12:36–37). It is important to notice that James is not calling here for silence only for control (see 1:19).

perfect. This same word is also used in 1:4 and 1:25. In all three instances, it is used to describe that which is mature, complete and whole. James is not teaching that Christians should be morally perfect, living in a state of sinlessness. This is obviously impossible. (See his words in this verse: "we all stumble," and in verse 8: "no man can tame the tongue.")

3:3–4 James now uses two metaphors to illustrate the point that he has just made that if a person controls his tongue, and "is never at fault in what he says," then that person is in control of his whole body. Both metaphors describe the power of the tongue.

3:3 horses. These huge, powerful animals can be controlled and guided by the human rider simply by means of a small bit.

3:4 ships. Ships were among the largest man-made objects that first-century people would have seen. That such a big structure driven by such powerful forces ("strong winds") could be controlled by so small a device as a rudder amply illustrates what James wants to say about the tongue. The person who controls the bit or rudder (or tongue) has control over the horse or ship (or the body).

3:5 it makes great boasts. Because of the good and evil for which it is responsible.

fire. During the dry season in Palestine, the scrub brush was apt to ignite easily and spread out of control. It only took a "small spark" to create a huge conflagration.

3:6 This is a notoriously difficult verse to translate or to understand. The general sense, however, is clear. The tongue is like a fire. It is capable of corrupting the whole person. Speech can burst forth into evil action.

a world of evil. As in 1:27, the "world" is that which stands in opposition to God. The tongue is, potentially, a force for evil. "The idea is, presumably, that it is in his speech that a man identifies himself with that total hostility to God, and shows that it is part of his inner character (cf. Mark 7:20)" (Laws).

hell. Literally *Gehenna*, a ravine south of Jerusalem where the garbage was burned. It became a metaphor for the place of punishment. These evil words find their inspiration and source in hell itself.

3:7–8 James pushes his case even further. Here he argues that, in fact, the tongue is basically evil.

3:7 tame. The Old Testament states that one of the functions of human beings is to domesticate the animal kingdom (see Gen. 1:28; 9:2; Psalm 8:6–8). Yet despite our ability to control all four classes of animals (mammals, birds, amphibians and fish), we remain unable to subdue our own tongues.

reptiles. In the Greco-Roman world, serpents were thought to have healing power, and so the ill slept among the tame snakes in the temples of Aesculapius. The modern symbol used by the medical profession has a snake entwined around a shaft.

3:8 restless. The same word is used in 1:8 and is translated there as "unstable." There it is used to describe the double-minded person. In 3:9 the dual nature of the tongue will be emphasized.

deadly poison. As with serpents, so too human tongues can bring death (see Psalm 58:3–5; 140:3).

3:9 with the tongue we praise. The tongue is vital to all worship: praying, singing, praising and thanking. Devout Jews offered praise to God three times a day.

curse men. It is by means of words that people bring real harm to others.

in God's likeness. Since people are made in the image of God, when they are cursed, God too is being cursed. The same tongue that praises God is also used to curse him, a point James makes explicit in verse 10.

3:11–12 James ends with three illustrations from nature which show how unnatural it is for human beings to use the same vehicle to utter praises and curses. Nothing in nature is like that, he says. A spring gives one type of water only: fresh water or brackish water. A tree bears only a single species of fruit.

UNIT 8—Two Kinds of Wisdom / James 3:13-18

Two Kinds of Wisdom

[13]Who is wise and understanding among you? Let him show it by his good life, by deeds done in the humility that comes from wisdom. [14]But if you harbor bitter envy and selfish ambition in your hearts, do not boast about it or deny the truth. [15]Such "wisdom" does not come down from heaven but is earthly, unspiritual, of the devil. [16]For where you have envy and selfish ambition, there you find disorder and every evil practice.

[17]But the wisdom that comes from heaven is first of all pure; then peace-loving, considerate, submissive, full of mercy and good fruit, impartial and sincere. [18]Peacemakers who sow in peace raise a harvest of righteousness.

READ

First Reading / First Impressions: If you had to make a bumper sticker out of this passage, what would you write?

Second Reading / Big Idea: What's the main point or topic?

SEARCH

1. How is someone with wisdom to be recognized (v. 13; see notes)?

2. What are two behaviors that indicate a lack of wisdom (v. 14)?

3. Where does such false "wisdom" originate (v. 15; see note)?

4. What two things happen as a result (v. 16)?

5. What are eight characteristics of real wisdom (v. 17)? With the help of the notes, write a brief definition or synonym.

6. What is the promise of a life given to peacemaking (v. 18)?

APPLY
List the seven characteristics of real wisdom from verse 17, and rate yourself on a scale from 1 to 10 (1 being low and 10 being high) in each of the categories.

CHARACTERISTICS	RATING

GROUP AGENDA

After the first part, read the Scripture out loud and divide into groups of 4. Then come back together for the third part.

TO BEGIN / 10–15 Min. (Choose 1 or 2)

1. Who deserved the Nobel Peace Prize in your family for knowing how to settle disputes between you and your sibling(s)?

2. Are you more likely to "say what you mean" (emphasis on correct speech), or "mean what you say" (emphasis on follow-up action)?

3. Who do you admire in your work or school for their ability to make wise decisions?

TO GO DEEPER / 30 Min. (Choose 2 or 3)

1. From the homework questions and the study notes, how do the two kinds of wisdom James writes about differ as to their source? Their symptoms? Their results?

2. Is the way of recognizing wisdom presented in this passage the way you usually judge wisdom?

3. What is the model here for effective managers, teachers, pastors and parents? For coworkers? For friends?

4. Where do you find it hardest to exercise "wisdom": At home? At work?

5. CASE STUDY: "If you can't take the heat, get out of the kitchen." This is the final word from your boss when he told you to cut your overhead by 10 percent and lay off two people. All of your staff have worked hard for you and all of them have a family to care for. How do you decide who to cut, and how do you go about telling them?

TO CLOSE / 15–30 Min.

1. Has your group assigned three people as a leadership core to start a new small group?

2. In the APPLY self-inventory, where did you mark yourself highest and lowest?

3. Has your spiritual life been more "God-centered" or more "you-centered" lately?

4. How would you like the group to pray for you this week?

NOTES

Summary. This is part two of James' discussion of wisdom. In it he probes why it is that, on the one hand, speech can be so destructive—yet on the other hand, there are teachers in the church (of which he is one) who communicate true wisdom. His conclusion is that it all depends on the source of the words. In this unit, he distinguishes between wisdom from above and wisdom from below. This unit not only looks backward to the problem of destructive speech (3:1–12), but it also looks forward to the problem such uncontrolled speech has brought to the Christian community—the issue James will deal with in the next section (4:1–12).

3:13 *Who is wise and understanding among you?* It might be anticipated that wisdom and understanding would be demonstrated by means of speech. Those who had the most understanding would possess the best verbal skills. They would be the popular teachers or the clever debaters. But this is not what James says. Understanding, like faith, is shown by *how one lives*. Specifically, understanding is demonstrated by a good life and by good deeds. Those who truly "understand" will live the kind of life that displays such understanding. "Lifestyle was absolutely critical for the early church. Elders were primarily examples (1 Tim. 4:12; 2 Tim. 3:10–11; 1 Peter 5:3), secondarily teachers: Their qualifications stress their exemplary lives and only mention their teaching ability as one item among many (1 Tim. 3; Titus 1)" (Davids, GNC).

humility. Contemporary Greek culture considered this to be a negative characteristic, fit only for slaves and characterized by abject grovelling. It was Christians who came to understand how crucial humility was for harmonious relationships (see Matt. 11:29; 2 Cor. 10:1; Phil. 2:8). A humble person will not need to make a point of how wise he or she is, and will not have to defend him/herself. Conflict is defused because the humble person has no need to establish a reputation over against other people. As James will show in 3:17–18, humility is also necessary for peace, which is itself a characteristic of true wisdom.

wisdom. These deeds arise not only from humility but also from wisdom, and so they display for all to see the fact of this inner understanding or wisdom.

3:14–16 Having described how true wisdom shows itself, James now turns to a description of how "pretend" wisdom displays itself. "His point is not that there is a different wisdom in opposition to the true one, but that a claim to true wisdom cannot be upheld in the context of an inconsistent style of life" (Laws).

3:14 Envy and ambition are the marks of false teachers. James is probably referring to the teachers he mentioned in 3:1 who are rivals vying for positions of authority within the Jerusalem church. Such competition clearly violates the nature of wisdom.

bitter envy. The word translated "bitter" is the same word which was used in verse 12 to describe brackish water unfit for human consumption.

selfish ambition. The word translated here as "selfish ambition" originally meant "those who can be hired to do spinning." Then it came to mean "those who work for pay." It later came to mean "those who work only for what they get out of it" and it was applied to those who sought political office merely for personal gain (Barclay).

in your hearts. This is the issue: What lies at the core of the person's being? Is it true wisdom from God or is it ambition? True wisdom will show itself via a good life filled with loving deeds done in a humble spirit. But envy and ambition will display itself by quite a different sort of life (see v. 16).

do not boast about it or deny the truth. Those whose hearts are filled with this sense of rivalry ought not to pretend that they are speaking God's wisdom. That is merely to compound the wrong.

3:15 James uses three terms—each of which is less desirable than the previous one—to describe the true origin of this "non-wisdom." There is "earthly" wisdom which arises out of this world. There is "unspiritual" wisdom which arises out of the "soul" of the person. Neither form of wisdom is necessarily bad, except when it claims to originate with the Spirit of God. And then there is wisdom "of the devil," which is not neutral. This phrase literally means "demon-like"; i.e., that which is possessed even by demons (see 2:19) or which is under the control of evil spirits.

3:16 James now defines the kind of life that emerges out of such pretend wisdom. It is a life of disorder and evil. The logic of what he says is quite clear. When personal ambition and a party spirit control the teaching in a church, then what is let loose in the community is disorder and evil, because peace and discipline are not present.

3:17–18 In contrast is the kind of personal and communal lifestyle that emerges out of wisdom from above. Here James gives a catalogue of the characteristics of such wisdom.

3:17 *wisdom.* "Nothing is said about an intellectual or doctrinal content for wisdom ... Wisdom is understood in terms of moral virtue and practical goodness" (Laws).

pure. The Greek word describes a sort of moral purity that enables one to approach the "gods." This is "wisdom which is so cleansed of all ulterior motives, so cleansed of self, that it has become pure enough to see God" (Barclay).

peace-loving. This is the opposite of envy and ambition. True wisdom produces right relationships between people, which is the root idea behind the word "peace" when it is used in the New Testament.

considerate. This is a very difficult word to translate into English. True wisdom will cause a person to be equitable and to make allowances, rather than always insisting in a harsh way on the letter of the law. At other places in the New Testament, this word is translated as "gentle."

submissive. Though this Greek word can be translated (as the NIV has done) to have the sense of "a willingness to obey God," it probably should be understood in its second sense of "willingness to be persuaded," since it follows the word "considerate." True wisdom is willing to listen, learn, and yield when persuaded.

full of mercy and good fruit. Christian mercy (compassion) is extended even to those whose troubles are their own fault, and is demonstrated by concrete action ("good fruit") and not just by an emotional response. True wisdom reaches out to the unfortunate in practical ways, a point James never tires of making.

impartial. Literally, "undivided." That is, true wisdom does not vacillate back and forth. It is the opposite of the wavering person in 1:6–8.

sincere. True wisdom does not act or pretend. It is honest and genuine.

3:18 "James argument ... runs as follows: There is not wisdom where there is divisiveness, for wisdom is peaceable; it is the peacemakers, then, who possess wisdom, which is the fruit of righteousness" (Laws). Peace flows from true wisdom, in contrast to the sort of harsh insistence on "truth" that divides people.

UNIT 9—Submit Yourselves to God / James 4:1-12

Submit Yourselves to God

4 **What causes fights and quarrels among you? Don't they come from your desires that battle within you? ²You want something but don't get it. You kill and covet, but you cannot have what you want. You quarrel and fight. You do not have, because you do not ask God. ³When you ask, you do not receive, because you ask with wrong motives, that you may spend what you get on your pleasures.**

⁴You adulterous people, don't you know that friendship with the world is hatred toward God? Anyone who chooses to be a friend of the world becomes an enemy of God. ⁵Or do you think Scripture says without reason that the spirit he caused to live in us envies intensely?ᵃ ⁶But he gives us more grace. That is why Scripture says:

"God opposes the proud
but gives grace to the humble."ᵇ

⁷Submit yourselves, then, to God. Resist the devil, and he will flee from you. ⁸Come near to God and he will come near to you. Wash your hands, you sinners, and purify your hearts, you double-minded. ⁹Grieve, mourn and wail. Change your laughter to mourning and your joy to gloom. ¹⁰Humble yourselves before the Lord, and he will lift you up.

¹¹Brothers, do not slander one another. Anyone who speaks against his brother or judges him speaks against the law and judges it. When you judge the law, you are not keeping it, but sitting in judgment on it. ¹²There is only one Lawgiver and Judge, the one who is able to save and destroy. But you—who are you to judge your neighbor?

ᵃ5 Or that God jealously longs for the spirit that he made to live in us; or that the Spirit he caused to live in us longs jealously
ᵇ6 Prov. 3:34

READ

First Reading / First Impressions: What's going on here? Check two:

- ❐ preaching
- ❐ comforting
- ❐ teaching
- ❐ pleading
- ❐ warning
- ❐ other:_____

Second Reading / Big Idea: If this was to be the sermon at your church this Sunday, what would be a good title for it (other than "Submit Yourselves to God")?

SEARCH

1. What is the root cause of fights and quarrels (v. 1; see notes)?

2. Why weren't these people getting what they wanted (v. 2)?

3. If our prayers are not answered, what could be the problem (v. 3; see notes)?

4. What two friendships are open to us (v. 4)? What does each mean?

5. What is James talking about when he calls these people "adulterous" (v. 4; see notes)?

6. What is God's attitude toward the proud and toward the humble (v. 6)?

7. What does it mean in your own words to submit to God, come near to God, and humble yourself before the Lord (vv. 7–10)?

8. What reasons does James give for not slandering or judging another (vv. 11–12; see notes)?

9. How does this passage compare to Jesus' teaching on murder in Matthew 5:21–22?

APPLY

Look at the 10 admonitions in verses 7–10 (see note on 4:7–10). In the space below, make some of them into a personal prayer of response. (For example: *Dear God, I submit myself—especially my attitude toward time and money—to you. ... I grieve about how little time I spend with you. ...*)

GROUP AGENDA

After the first part, read the Scripture out loud and divide into groups of 4. Then come back together for the third part.

TO BEGIN / 10–15 Min. (Choose 1 or 2)
1. Who did you quarrel with most when you were growing up?

2. What did you quarrel over?

3. What purchase is highest on your "wish list" right now?

TO GO DEEPER / 30 Min. (Choose 2 or 3)
1. What did you find out from the homework questions and study notes about our desires and why we don't always get what we want? What else stood out to you from READ or SEARCH?

2. How do you usually react when you don't get something you want?

3. What happens to relationships when we covet?

4. What is "friendship with the world"? How are you most likely to fall into loyalty to this "friend": Lifestyle? Image? Pleasures of money or things?

5. Are Christians supposed to look like verse 9? When is this behavior right and necessary?

6. CASE STUDY: John, your friend, is caught up in the rat race—climbing the ladder at work and keeping up with the Joneses at church. Recently, he has had trouble with ulcers and last week his partner died of a heart attack at age 38. John is really shaken up. What can you say to help him?

TO CLOSE / 15–30 Min.
1. How are you doing on your group mission?

2. How "near" (v. 8) do you feel to God right now? How does that compare to six months ago?

3. What prayer concerns do you have for the group?

4. Close by inviting group members to read the prayers they wrote for the APPLY exercise.

NOTES

Summary. This is the third and final part of James' discussion about wisdom. Here he applies his insights to the question of their community life together as a church. Their failure to live out God's wisdom has had the most serious consequences for them as a church. In the previous section (3:13–18) he mentioned in a general way the disorder and evil that came from envy and ambition. Now he gets quite specific.

4:1–3 James begins by naming the root cause of all this strife. It is the desire for pleasure.

4:1 *fights and quarrels.* Literally, "wars and battles." These are long-term conflicts, not sudden explosions.

desires. Literally, "pleasures." In Greek the word is *hedone*, from which our word "hedonism" is derived. James is not saying that personal pleasure is inherently wrong. However, there is a certain desire for gratification that springs from the wrong source and seems to possess a person in the pursuit for its fulfillment.

battle. The human personality is pictured as having been invaded by an alien army. "Human nature is indeed in the grip of an overwhelming army of occupation. Its natural aim, it can be truthfully said, is pleasure; and when we consider the amount of time, energy, money, interest and enthusiasm that men and women give to the satisfaction of this aim we can appreciate the accuracy of James' diagnosis; and Christians can use it as a reliable yardstick by which to measure the sincerity of their religion. Is God or pleasure the dominant concern of their life" (Tasker)?

within you. The struggle is within a person between the part of him or her which is controlled by the Holy Spirit and that which is controlled by the world.

4:2 *You want something.* This is desire at work (see 1:14).

but don't get it. This is desire frustrated.

kill and covet. This is how frustrated desire responds. It lashes out at others in anger and abuse. (This "killing" is in a metaphorical sense—see Matt. 5:21–22.) It responds in jealousy to those who have what it wants.

quarrel and fight. But still they do not have what they desire, so the hostile action continues. The point is that this mad desire-driven quest causes a person to disregard other people, trampling over them if necessary to get what is wanted.

you do not ask God. One reason for this frustrated desire is a lack of prayer.

4:3 James senses a protest: "But I did ask God and I didn't get it." So he qualifies the absolute assertion in verse 2. The desire expressed in prayer may be inappropriate. God will not grant this type of request. Christians pray "in the name of Jesus," implying submission to the will of God. They can ask for wisdom and always expect to get it (if they do not waver), as James explains in 1:5. But this is quite different than asking for something to satisfy an illicit pleasure and always expecting to get it. Prayer is not magic.

spend. This is the same word used in Luke 15:14 to describe the profligate behavior of the Prodigal Son.

4:4–6 To pray with wrong motives so as to fulfill one's illegitimate pleasures is a sign of friendship with the world.

4:4 adulterous people. In Greek, this word is feminine, *adulteresses*, and probably refers to the people of Israel. By extension it refers to the church, the new Israel. In the Old Testament it was common to picture the relationship between God and his people as similar to the relationship between a husband and his wife (see Isa. 54:5). To give spiritual allegiance to another ("the world") is therefore expressed in terms of adultery.

don't you know. This is not a new teaching for them. They were aware that this was not the way to live.

friendship with the world. Rather than living in God's way, in the light of God's wisdom, his people are being molded by the values and desires of secular culture. They have, as it were, crossed over into the enemy's camp and decided to live there.

4:5 This is a most difficult verse to translate, as the footnote in the NIV text indicates. There is a further problem: It is not clear to which verse in Scripture James is referring. Perhaps it is just an allusion to what Scripture says in general about jealousy. In any case, this verse would stand as a warning that what they are doing by forming this allegiance with the world is very dangerous.

4:6 But their case is not hopeless. God does give grace. Repentance is possible. They can turn from their misbehavior.

4:7–10 James now tells them how to repent by means of a series of 10 commands. He has switched to the imperative voice: "Do this," he says, "and you will escape the mess you have gotten yourselves in." He tells them to submit, resist, come near, wash, purify, grieve, mourn, wail, change, and humble themselves.

4:7 Submit yourselves, then, to God. His first and primary command is that they must submit to God. It is not too surprising that James says this, since what these Christians have been doing is resisting God and his ways. As James just pointed out, it is the humble who receive God's grace. A proud person is unwilling to submit and therefore not open to grace, feeling that he or she needs nothing.

Resist the devil. Submission to God begins with resistance to Satan. Thus far they have been giving in to the devil's enticements. A clear sign of their new lifestyle will be this inner resistance to devilish desires.

he will flee from you. Since Satan has no ultimate power over a Christian, when resisted he can do little but withdraw.

4:9 True repentance will often show itself in strong feelings of grief. James is not urging asceticism as a lifestyle. Rather, he is teaching about the dynamics of repentance (see Jer. 4:8 and Joel 2:12–14).

Grieve. This word originally described "the experience of an army whose food has gone and who have no shelter for the stormy weather" (Barclay).

mourn and wail. When people realize that they have been leading self-centered lives, in disobedience to God and harmful to others, they often feel overwhelming grief at what they have done.

4:10 Humble. This last command urges humility before God as did the first command ("Submit to God").

4:11–12 James ends his section on wisdom and speech by moving from a general call to repentance (vv. 7–10) to a specific form of wrongdoing that they must deal with. His focus is on the sin of judgment and the pride that underlies it.

slander. This is to speak evil about other people in their absence so that they are unable to defend themselves. The word means both *false* accusation and harsh (though perhaps accurate) *criticism*.

speaks against the law. When a person judges someone else, it is a violation of the royal law of love (2:8) and thus a criticism of that law because of the implicit assumption that it is not fully true since it does not apply in this case.

UNIT 10—Boasting About Tomorrow / James 4:13–17

Boasting About Tomorrow

¹³Now listen, you who say, "Today or tomorrow we will go to this or that city, spend a year there, carry on business and make money." ¹⁴Why, you do not even know what will happen tomorrow. What is your life? You are a mist that appears for a little while and then vanishes. ¹⁵Instead, you ought to say, "If it is the Lord's will, we will live and do this or that." ¹⁶As it is, you boast and brag. All such boasting is evil. ¹⁷Anyone, then, who knows the good he ought to do and doesn't do it, sins.

READ

First Reading / First Impressions: How would this go over today as a speech to the local chamber of commerce?

Second Reading / Big Idea: James is:
- ❐ against planning
- ❐ rebuking the rich
- ❐ advocating dependence on God
- ❐ other:_____

SEARCH

1. What are the four agendas that characterize the lifestyle of the merchants in verse 13 (see notes)?

2. To what extent has this agenda been your approach to life?

3. How does James look upon life and caution us about these agendas (v. 14; see notes)?

4. In contrast to the arrogant statement in verse 13, how should a Christian think (v. 15; see notes)?

48

5. What is wrong with the opposite lifestyle (v. 16)?

6. In your own words, state the spiritual principle or teaching in verse 17 (see notes). Use your own everyday speech and personal situation.

APPLY

Think of the next six months of your life and jot down three goals that you feel would be in keeping with the teaching in this passage. Then, in the right column, jot down a word of caution for each goal. For example: GOAL: to take a night course; CAUTION: not to reduce family time.

THREE GOALS	THREE CAUTIONS

GROUP AGENDA

After the first part, read the Scripture out loud and divide into groups of 4. Then come back together for the third part.

TO BEGIN / 10–15 Min. (Choose 1 or 2)

1. When you play games like Monopoly, do you "play it safe" or "go for broke"?

2. When you were 15, what did you expect to be doing at age 25? Were you right?

3. Are you a long-range planner or a "one day at a time" person?

TO GO DEEPER / 30 Min. (Choose 2 or 3)

1. Based on the homework questions and reference notes, how would you describe James' perspective on life in general, and toward the future in particular?

2. How often is your outlook like this? Would you say that you have the proper balance between planning ahead and living one day at a time?

3. How should a Christian's lifestyle and prayer life reflect verse 15?

4. How did you restate the principle of verse 17 in #6 of SEARCH? What "sins of omission" of your own are you most aware of?

5. CASE STUDY: Your uncle started out as a Fuller brush salesman. Then he got his own business and traveled the world making money. He owns three houses, his own airplane and a yacht in Florida. Now that he "has it all," he's bored and feels bad about ignoring his children while they were growing up. What is your advice for your uncle now?

TO CLOSE / 15–30 Min.

1. How did your group answer the three "Brainstorming" questions on page M19 in the center section?

2. What did you write in the goal-setting exercise in APPLY?

3. How can the group pray for you?

NOTES

Summary. James begins discussion of his third and final theme: testing. He will deal with this theme, at first, as it touches the issue of wealth. He has just spoken about a particular form of disharmony within the Christian community, that which is generated by slander and judgment (4:11–12). Now he turns to a different problem: the difficulty that comes from being wealthy and the kind of problems this brings, both on a personal level and for the whole community. In this first part of his discussion (4:13–17), he looks at the situation of a group of Christian businessmen—in particular, at their "sins of omission."

4:13 Boasting about what will happen tomorrow is another example of human arrogance. It is in the same category as judging one another (vv. 11–12). Judgment is arrogant because God is the only legitimate judge. Boasting about the future is arrogant because God is the only one who knows what will happen in the future. Such arrogance is the opposite of humility, which is supposed to characterize Christians (v. 10). It is also another sign of "friendship with the world" (v. 4).

Now listen. This is literally "Come now." It stands in sharp contrast to the way James has been addressing his readers. In the previous section he called them "my brothers" (3:1,11). James reverts to this more impersonal language in addressing these merchants.

"Today or tomorrow we will go ... " James lets us listen in on the plans of a group of businessmen. Possibly they are looking at a map together. In any case, they are planning for the future and are concerned with where they will go, how long they will stay, what they will do, and how much profit they will make. It appears to be an innocent conversation. "In trade a person has to plan ahead: Travel plans, market projections, time frames, profit forecasts are the stuff of business in all ages. Every honest merchant would plan in exactly the same way—pagan, Jew or Christian—and that is exactly the problem James has with these plans: There is absolutely nothing about their desires for the future, their use of money, or their way of doing business that is any different from the rest of the world. Their worship may be exemplary, their personal morality, impeccable; but when it comes to business they think entirely on a worldly plane" (Davids, GNC).

we will go. Travel by traders in the first century usually took the form of caravan or ship. There were no hard and fast time tables. Instead, one had to wait until the right transportation came along going in your direction. However, there were certain seasons when ships sailed and caravans were more likely to travel.

carry on business. The word James uses here is derived from the Greek word *emporos*, from which the English word "emporium" comes. It denotes wholesale merchants who traveled from city to city, buying and selling. A different word was used to describe local peddlers who had small businesses in the bazaars. The growth of cities and the increase of trade between them during the Greco-Roman era created great opportunities for making money. In the Bible a certain distrust of traders is sometimes expressed (see Prov. 20:23; Amos 8:4–6; Rev. 18:11–20).

4:14 ***tomorrow.*** All such planning presupposes that tomorrow will unfold like any other day, when in fact the future is anything but secure (see Prov. 27:1).

What is your life? Is it not death that is the great unknown? Who can know when death will come and interrupt plans? "Their projections are made; their plans are laid. But it all hinges on a will higher than theirs, a God unconsulted in their planning. That very night disease might strike; suddenly their plans evaporate, their only trip being one on a bier to a cold grave. They are like the rich fool of Jesus' parable, who had made a large honest profit through the chance occurrences of farming. Feeling secure, he makes rational plans for a comfortable retirement. But God said to him, "You fool! This very night you will have to give up your life" (Luke 12:16–21). By thinking on the worldly plane, James' Christian business people have gained a false sense of security. They need to look death in the face and realize their lack of control over life" (Davids, GNC).

mist. Hosea 13:3 says, "Therefore they will be like the morning mist, like the early dew that disappears, like chaff swirling from a threshing floor, like smoke escaping through a window."

4:15 ***"If it is the Lord's will."*** This phrase (often abbreviated D.V. after its Latin form) is not used in the Old Testament, though it was found frequently in Greek and Roman literature and is used by Paul (see Acts 18:21; 1 Cor. 4:19; 16:7). The uncertainty of the future ought not to be a terror to the Christian. Instead, it ought to force on him or her an awareness of how dependent a person is upon God, and thus move that person to planning that involves God.

we will live and do this or that. James is not ruling out planning. He says plan, but keep God in mind.

4:16 In contrast to such prayerful planning, these Christian merchants are very proud of what they do on their own. James is not condemning international trade as such, nor the wealth it produced. (His comments on riches come in 5:1–3.) What he is concerned about is that all this is done without reference to God, in a spirit of boastful arrogance.

boast. The problem with this boasting is that they are claiming to have the future under control when, in fact, it is God who holds time in his hands. These are empty claims.

brag. This word originally described an itinerant quack who touted "cures" that did not work. It came to mean claiming to be able to do something you could not do.

4:17 Some feel that this proverb-like statement may, in fact, be a saying of Jesus that did not get recorded in the Gospel accounts. In any case, by it James points out the nature of so-called "sins of omission." In other words, it is sin when we fail to do what we ought to do. The more familiar definition is of "sins of commission" or wrongdoing (see 1 John 3:4). In other words, sinning can be both active and passive. Christians can sin by doing what they ought not to do (law-breaking); or by not doing what they know they should do (failure).

who knows the good. James applies this principle to these merchants. It is not that they are cheating and stealing in the course of their business (that would be active wrongdoing). The problem is what they fail to do. Generally James defines "the good" as acts of charity toward those in need. And certainly in the context of this letter, it would appear that these men are failing in their duty to the poor. "James, then, may be suggesting that they plan like the world because they are motivated by the world, for God has his own way to invest money: give it to the poor (Matt. 6:19–21). If they took God into account they might not be trying to increase their own standard of living; God might lead them to relieve the suffering around them, that is, to do good" (Davids, GNC).

UNIT 11—Warning to Rich Oppressors / James 5:1-6

Warning to Rich Oppressors

5 Now listen, you rich people, weep and wail because of the misery that is coming upon you. ²Your wealth has rotted, and moths have eaten your clothes. ³Your gold and silver are corroded. Their corrosion will testify against you and eat your flesh like fire. You have hoarded wealth in the last days. ⁴Look! The wages you failed to pay the workmen who mowed your fields are crying out against you. The cries of the harvesters have reached the ears of the Lord Almighty. ⁵You have lived on earth in luxury and self-indulgence. You have fattened yourselves in the day of slaughter.ᵃ ⁶You have condemned and murdered innocent men, who were not opposing you.

ᵃ5 Or *yourselves as in a day of feasting*

READ

First Reading / First Impressions: Complete this sentence: James ...

- ❑ is anti-capitalism.
- ❑ would be crucified on Wall Street.
- ❑ ought to run for president.
- ❑ makes me mad!
- ❑ other:_____

Second Reading / Big Idea: What feelings rise in you as you read this? Why?

SEARCH

1. To whom is this passage addressed (v. 1; see "Summary" in the notes)?

2. What is going to happen to these people (v. 1; see notes for v. 1)?

3. From the three indictments against the rich, what do you learn about the source of their wealth and what is happening to each commercial enterprise (vv. 2–3)?

SOURCE OF WEALTH   **CALAMITY**

4. What is the bigger crisis that the rich will face in the future (v. 3; see notes)?

5. In obtaining wealth, what are three abuses they have committed (vv. 4–6; see notes)?

APPLY

In the area of abusing wealth, try to summarize the ideas in this passage for a contemporary audience. Keep in mind that the world this was written to was basically a two-class system—the rich and the poor—somewhat like many underdeveloped countries today. What is the message here for *your* culture? (For example, complete sentences like: *About materialism, James would say ... . About labor / management relations, James would say ... .*)

GROUP AGENDA

After the first part, read the Scripture out loud and divide into groups of 4. Then come back together for the third part.

TO BEGIN / 10–15 Min. (Choose 1 or 2)

1. If you won the lottery, what would you do with your first $100,000?

2. When have you held a job in which you were underpaid?

3. When have you made a purchase, only to regret it later?

TO GO DEEPER / 30 Min. (Choose 2 or 3)

1. What did you learn from the homework questions and study notes about who this passage was directed to, what they were guilty of, and what they have to look forward to?

2. Do you believe the rich abuse the poor today? If so, how?

3. Do you think the church should get involved in or speak out against social and political abuses? If so, how?

4. What do you think James would say about the concerns most people have today for saving money, preparing for retirement, estate planning, etc.?

5. Would James say that you "have hoarded wealth," failed to fairly "pay the workmen," and/or "lived on earth in luxury and self-indulgence"?

6. CASE STUDY: The youth director took a group of youth from your church to Haiti where they were appalled by the poverty and social injustice. They first started raising funds to send to Haiti, but now they want to boycott products and send a petition to an American corporation that exploits the situation. One of the board members of your church is a stockholder in that company. What do you say as a fellow member of the board?

TO CLOSE / 15–30 Min.

1. What did you write in APPLY?

2. How could your church use its resources, property and influence to help overcome the problems in your community?

3. What is one thing you could personally do to "light a candle rather than curse the darkness"?

4. How would you like the group to pray?

NOTES

Summary. James is still on the theme of wealth, but now he shows that riches are, indeed, a great burden when seen in eternal terms. In an unusually vivid passage, James points out the ultimate worthlessness of wealth in the face of the coming judgment. Although he is addressing the rich directly, he is also warning Christians not to covet wealth. Wealth is an illusion. It gives one a false sense of security. Not only that, it is gained at the expense of the poor, even to the extent of depriving them of their lives. And all this so that the rich can live in self-indulgent ways. In the previous passage James was concerned with the merchant class, business people who were, in this case, Christians (4:13–17). In this passage, his focus is on the landowner class who were, by and large, non-Christians.

5:1 *Now listen.* James continues his impersonal mode of address. See the note on 4:13.

rich people. In the first century there was a great gulf between rich and poor. Whereas a poor laborer (as in verse 4) might have received one denarius a day as wages (see Matt. 20:2,9), a rich widow was said to have cursed the scribes because they allowed her only 400 gold denari a day to spend on luxuries! In the face of such extravagance, the words of James take on new meaning (see Matt. 6:19–21,24; Mark 10:17–31; Luke 6:24). Peter Davids argues that the people in view here are wealthy non-Christians since James seems to reserve the word "rich" for those outside the Christian community (see 1:10 and 2:6).

weep. James says that the appropriate response for these wealthy non-Christians is tears. Their luxury is only for the moment. In contrast, in 1:2 and 1:12, he urged the poor Christians to rejoice because their present suffering will pass, bringing with it great reward.

wail. This is a strong word meaning "to shriek" or "howl," and is used to describe the terror that will be felt by the damned (see Isa. 13:6; 14:31; Amos 8:3).

the misery that is coming. James is referring to the future Day of Judgment, an event that will take place when the Lord returns. The noun *misery* is related (in the Greek) to the verb *grieve* used in 4:9. However, there is an important difference between the two uses. In 4:9 the grieving was self-imposed, the result of seeing one's failure, and it had a good result. Repentance opened up one to grace. But here this wretchedness results from the horror of being judged.

5:2–3 James points to the three major forms of wealth in the first century—food, clothes and precious metals—and describes the decay of each. Agricultural products like corn and oil will rot. Clothes will become moth-eaten. Even previous metal will corrode.

5:2 clothes. Garments were one of the main forms of wealth in the first century. They were used as a means of payment, given as gifts, and passed on to one's children (see Gen. 45:22; Josh. 7:21; Judges 14:12; 2 Kings 5:5; Acts 20:33).

5:3 corroded. Pure gold and silver do not rust or corrode (though silver will tarnish). James is using hyperbole to make his point: no form of wealth will make a person immune from the final judgment.

testify against you. The existence of rotten food, moth-eaten garments and rusty coins will stand as a condemnation against the person. Instead of being stored, these goods should have been used to feed and clothe the poor.

eat your flesh like fire. In a striking image, James pictures wealth as having now turned against the person and become part of the torment he or she must endure. Just as rust eats through metal, so too it will eat through the flesh of the rich (see Luke 16:19–31 and Mark 9:43).

the last days. The early Christians felt that Jesus would return very shortly, to draw his people to himself and to establish his kingdom on earth. James' point is: how inappropriate it is to give your energies over to accumulating treasures when, in effect, time itself is drawing to a close. This is an example of the kind of arrogance and pride that plans boldly for the future as if a person could control what lies ahead (see 4:14–16). "The rich gather and invest as if they or their descendants will live forever, yet the last days, the beginning of the end, are already here. James sees as tragic figures well-dressed men and women pondering investments over excellent meals; they act as if they were winners, but in reality have lost the only game that matters" (Davids, GNC).

5:4–6 James now gets very specific as he details just how it is that these folks were able to accumulate such wealth. In particular he points to the injustices leveled against those who worked on the farms.

5:4 Look! James will not let them turn away from this stinging condemnation. They must see things

as they are. They must face the reality of their own injustice.

wages you failed to pay. If a laborer was not given his wages at the end of the day, his family would go hungry the next day. The Old Testament insists that it is wrong to withhold wages. A worker was to be paid immediately. "Despite a host of Old Testament laws (Lev. 19:13; Deut. 24:14–15), ways were found to withhold payments (e.g., Jer. 22:13; Mal. 3:5). One might withhold them until the end of the harvest season to keep the worker coming back, grasp at a technicality to show that the contract was not fulfilled, or just be too tired to pay that night. If the poor worker complained, the landlord could blacklist him; if he went to court the rich had the better lawyers. James pictures the money in the pockets of the rich, money that should have been paid to the laborers, crying out for justice" (Davids, GNC).

the workman. In Palestine, day laborers were used to plant and harvest the crops. They were cheaper than slaves, since if a slave converted to Judaism, he or she had to be freed in the sabbatical year.

fields. The Greek word means "estates." These were the large tracts of land owned by the very wealthy.

crying out. This is a word used to describe the wild, incoherent cry of an animal.

the Lord Almighty. Literally, "The Lord of Sabaoth" or "Lord of Hosts," i.e., the commander of the heavenly armies. This is an unusual title, found at only one other place in the New Testament (and there it is a quote—Rom. 9:29). James has probably drawn the title from Isaiah 5:7,9,16,24—a chapter whose concerns parallel his own in this passage.

5:5 luxury. In contrast to the hunger of the laborers is the soft living of the landowners (see Amos 6:1–7).

self-indulgence. "To live in lewdness and lasciviousness and wanton riotousness" (Barclay). Not just luxury but vice is in view here.

day of slaughter. Cattle were pampered and fattened for one purpose only: to be slaughtered. On the day when this took place a great feast was held.

5:6 There is yet another accusation against the rich—they use their wealth and power to oppress the poor even to the point of death (see Amos 5:11–12; 8:4–6).

UNIT 12—Patience in Suffering / James 5:7–12

Patience in Suffering

⁷Be patient, then, brothers, until the Lord's coming. See how the farmer waits for the land to yield its valuable crop and how patient he is for the autumn and spring rains. ⁸You too, be patient and stand firm, because the Lord's coming is near. ⁹Don't grumble against each other, brothers, or you will be judged. The Judge is standing at the door!

¹⁰Brothers, as an example of patience in the face of suffering, take the prophets who spoke in the name of the Lord. ¹¹As you know, we consider blessed those who have persevered. You have heard of Job's perseverance and have seen what the Lord finally brought about. The Lord is full of compassion and mercy.

¹²Above all, my brothers, do not swear—not by heaven or by earth or by anything else. Let your "Yes" be yes, and your "No," no, or you will be condemned.

READ

First Reading / First Impressions: James' advice here:

❐ would only encourage the rich to oppress even more
❐ seems to accept injustice
❐ gives the poor hope
❐ other:_____

Second Reading / Big Idea: How would you sum up this passage in one sentence?

SEARCH

1. What is the most repeated word in this passage? Who is James speaking to?

2. What are they called upon to wait for (v. 7)?

3. What does the illustration of the crops and the rain teach (vv. 7–8; see notes)?

4. What should Christians do while waiting for the Second Coming (v. 8; see note)?

5. What should they *not* do (v. 9; see note)?

6. Why (v. 9)?

7. From your knowledge of the Old Testament, give an example of a prophet James may be thinking of in verses 10–11?

8. What is the point of the Job illustration (v. 11; see notes)?

9. What are Christians to guard against (v. 12; see note)?

APPLY

Make a study of Christian mental attitudes in this passage. Jot down all words or phrases that describe an attitude or behavior in this passage, along with the reference. On a scale from 1 (low) to 10 (high), how are you doing in these areas?

VERSE	MENTAL ATTITUDE / BEHAVIOR	RATING

GROUP AGENDA

After the first part, read the Scripture out loud and divide into groups of 4. Then come back together for the third part.

TO BEGIN / 10–15 Min. (Choose 1 or 2)

1. Who are you closer to today because you went through a difficult time together?

2. Have you ever tried to raise a garden or crop and felt like the crop would never ripen?

3. What do you hate waiting for?

TO GO DEEPER / 30 Min. (Choose 2 or 3)

1. As Christians, what are we waiting for? From the homework questions and study notes, what do you learn about how we should live while we're waiting?

2. Have you ever gone through a period when you doubted God's presence in the midst of hardship or suffering? How do you look back upon these times now?

3. How do James' illustrations—the farmer, the prophets and Job—bring encouragement?

4. How are you at keeping your word—letting your "Yes" be yes, and your "No," no? How seriously do you take sincerity and follow-through in your commitments?

5. How much does the anticipation of the Lord's coming influence or affect your behavior and lifestyle right now?

6. CASE STUDY: Your friend has been out of work for nearly a year. He has a good attitude, but signs of strain are beginning to show on him and his wife. How could you be of help?

TO CLOSE / 15–30 Min.

1. Are you planning a kickoff for starting a new small group? Have you made plans for celebrating your time together as a group?

2. How did you fill out the exercise in APPLY?

3. In this passage, the prophets were affirmed for their patience and Job was affirmed for his perseverance. How would you affirm the person on your left? Go around the group doing so.

4. What's something in your life for which you've been waiting a long time? How can the group join you in prayer?

NOTES

Summary. James' argument is finished. He has said what he wants to say about testing (and temptation), about wisdom (and speech), and about riches (and generosity). Now all that remains is for him to conclude his book by summarizing his points. However, he does not do this in a neat systematic way. Rather, he simply alludes to each theme in the midst of offering final encouragement to the church in its struggles. So, in 5:7–11, he touches on the theme of trials by way of rounding off his discussion of riches. In 5:1–6 he had some harsh things to say to the opulently wealthy. Here he has some encouraging things to say to those who have been abused by the wealthy. In so doing he tells them not to grumble—this is an inappropriate form of speech. In 5:12 he again touches on the theme of speech by warning against the use of oaths. Then in 5:13–17, it is back to the idea of trials, but this time it is in the context of illness. "Pray," he says, "ask God for health"; and so he interweaves the idea of speech (prayer) and wisdom ("ask God"). His concluding words in 5:19–20 identify his reason for writing the book in the first place: to bring wandering believers back to God's way of truth.

5:7–8 James begins this concluding section by summarizing his ideas about testing.

5:7 *patient.* This word (and its derivatives) are the most frequently used words in the passage. The basic idea is that of patient waiting. It is related to the endurance that James commended in 1:3 ("perseverance"), though patience connotes a more passive holding on than the active endurance of chapter 1. This word carries with it the idea of "self-restraint in the face of injustice" like that which he catalogued in 5:4–6 (failure to be paid, being used to bring opulence to a few while personally being forced to live in poverty, abuse in the courts, murder). The opposite response to such patience would be retaliation or vengeance (see Rom. 2:4 and 1 Peter 3:20).

brothers. James has shifted back into this personal form of address (as in 4:11 and elsewhere), away from his impersonal tone in 4:13 and 5:1. The whole atmosphere of the passage has changed from that of warning and command (in 4:13–5:6) to encouragement and gentle instruction.

until. Such patient waiting on the part of the poor is possible because they know an event is coming that will radically change their situation—the Lord's return.

the Lord's coming. There are three words in the New Testament used to describe the Second Coming of Jesus. The first is *epiphaneia* (English: "epiphany"). It describes the appearance of a god or the ascent to the throne of an emperor (see 2 Tim. 4:1). The second word is *apokalupsis* (English: apocalypse) and means "unveiling" or "revelation" (see 1 Peter 1:7,13). The third word—which is used here—is *parousia*. It describes the invasion of a country or the arrival of a king (Barclay). Taken together, these three words give the sense of what will occur when Christ returns. Jesus first came to this planet in secret as a little baby in Bethlehem. When he comes a second time it will be in great and obvious power as the rightful King. In great glory he will ascend his throne and claim his people.

See how the farmer waits. In due course, the rains will come. In the meantime, the farmer can do nothing to hasten or delay their arrival. He must simply wait for the gift of rain.

for the land to yield. Likewise, he must wait for the land to give forth a crop. Once he has sowed his seed, apart from pulling out weeds and keeping birds and animals away, there is nothing the farmer can do. Growth, too, is a gift.

valuable. This was literally his most precious possession. Without a crop he would have nothing to sell or barter. Even worse, he and his family would starve.

rains. The fall rain was necessary to prepare the hard ground for sowing and to enable the seed to germinate. The spring rains were vital for the grain to ripen and mature. "All this time his food supplies were getting lower; it was not uncommon for food to be rationed and the children to be crying from hunger during the month or two before harvest. The later the rains, the worse it was. But with his life in his hands he had to wait for conditions outside his control" (Davids, GNC; see also Deut. 11:14; Jer. 5:24 and Joel 2:23).

5:8 You, too. There is a lesson for Christians found in the experience of the farmer. They too must wait. Their fate too is in the hands of an event which they can do nothing to bring about.

stand firm. But while waiting, the temptation will be to slip into inappropriate survival modes of adopting the methods of the world (e.g., revenge). The longer they wait, the stronger the temptation to doubt the Second Coming, and even to doubt the Christian faith itself. They must resist these temptations.

5:9 James now touches on the theme of speech.

grumble. This word is literally "groan." While groaning in the face of suffering is appropriate (see Mark 7:34 and Rom. 8:23), groaning at one another is not! While they wait, they are not to bicker and find fault. Such grumbling can easily develop when people cannot vent their frustrations at those causing the problem, so it is directed at those who are around them.

you will be judged. Grumbling against others is a form of judgment so this reference may be to the teaching of Jesus: "Do not judge." This is likely since James frequently refers to the Sermon on the Mount. Or James may have in mind the Day of Judgment which will occur at the Second Coming.

Judge. Jesus will return to judge all.

at the door. This is a phrase used by Jesus himself to convey a sense of immediacy concerning the Second Coming (see Mark 13:29).

5:10–11 From the theme of speech, James moves back to the theme of trials and tests.

5:11 persevered. At this point, James shifts from the more passive word "patience" to the idea of active endurance of suffering, a concept which describes Job's experience (see 1:3; Matt. 10:22; 24:13; Luke 21:19; 1 Cor. 9:24–27; Phil. 3:13–14).

Job. The book of Job details the experience of this man: his illness, poverty, misunderstanding, and loss of family. Despite all this, Job does not lose his faith in God (Job 13:15; 16:19–21; 19:25). This is an apt illustration since Job's experience paralleled their experience at many points.

finally brought about. But in the end, God blessed Job with far more than he had at the beginning of his trials (Job 42:10–17). The implications of this are clear: if they will hold on ("stand firm"), their reward too will be great.

5:12 swear. The issue is not that of using foul language, but of taking an oath to guarantee a promise. The extraordinary amount of oath-taking in those days was an indication of how widespread lying and cheating was. (Honest people need no oaths.) In Jewish society, an oath containing the name of God was binding, since God was then seen as a partner in the transaction. But when God's name was not mentioned, the oath was not binding. Christians are to be people of their word, not like the people of the world who used (abused) words to get their own way.

UNIT 13—The Prayer of Faith / James 5:13–20

The Prayer of Faith

¹³*Is any one of you in trouble? He should pray. Is anyone happy? Let him sing songs of praise.* ¹⁴*Is any one of you sick? He should call the elders of the church to pray over him and anoint him with oil in the name of the Lord.* ¹⁵*And the prayer offered in faith will make the sick person well; the Lord will raise him up. If he has sinned, he will be forgiven.* ¹⁶*Therefore confess your sins to each other and pray for each other so that you may be healed. The prayer of a righteous man is powerful and effective.*

¹⁷*Elijah was a man just like us. He prayed earnestly that it would not rain, and it did not rain on the land for three and a half years.* ¹⁸*Again he prayed, and the heavens gave rain, and the earth produced its crops.*

¹⁹*My brothers, if one of you should wander from the truth and someone should bring him back,* ²⁰*remember this: Whoever turns a sinner from the error of his way will save him from death and cover over a multitude of sins.*

READ

First Reading / First Impressions: What do you see as two or three key words here?

Second Reading / Big Idea: What is a central attitude that James encourages here?

SEARCH

1. What should Christians do when in trouble (v. 13)?

2. When happy (v. 13)?

3. When sick (v. 14)?

4. When they have sinned (v. 16; see notes)?

5. What does the example of Elijah teach (vv. 17–18; see notes)?

6. What is the responsibility of Christians to those who leave Christian truth (v. 19)?

7. What two blessings will this bring (v. 20)?

APPLY
Read through this passage again, looking for ways it relates personally to your life (or to someone close to you). Write down those situations—for example, your own anxieties or physical ailment or a friend who has strayed from the Christian faith—along with any admonition or encouragement from the passage. Finally, record any commitment you want to make in this regard. Sharing in the group meeting what you write will be optional.

GROUP AGENDA

After the first part, read the Scripture out loud and divide into groups of 4. Then come back together for the third part.

TO BEGIN / 10–15 Min. (Choose 1 or 2)

1. As a child, did you pray before bed? If so, do you remember the prayer—or did you pray spontaneously each night?

2. When have you experienced drought or too much rain? How long did the effects last?

3. What is the sickest you have ever been? How long did it take you to heal?

TO GO DEEPER / 30 Min. (Choose 2 or 3)

1. How likely are you to pray when you are in trouble, and to sing when you are happy?

2. What is the connection between the spiritual, emotional, physical, vocational and relational areas in our lives? Can you be sick in one area and completely whole in the others?

3. From the homework and study notes, what stands out to you about how the body of Christ participates in the ministry of healing for one another?

4. How do you feel about "calling for the elders" when you are sick? How do you feel about trying to "bring back" one who has "wandered from the truth"?

5. When have you come the closest to wandering from the faith? What (or who) helped bring you back?

6. CASE STUDY: Bob ran away from home and joined the army 20 years ago. His father was an alcoholic and abused him as a child. Bob has made his peace with God, but not with his family. In fact, he has not seen his family for 20 years. What would you suggest Bob do?

TO CLOSE / 15–30 Min.

1. Would you like to share what you wrote in APPLY? (This is definitely optional.)

2. What have you appreciated about this course and this group?

3. Have you finalized your plans for the future of your group?

4. What would you like to praise God for as you pray together? How can this group continue praying for you?

NOTES

Summary. In literary epistles such as this one, according to Peter Davids, it is customary to end with three items: an oath, a health wish, and the purpose for writing. James has each of these. In verse 12, oaths are mentioned (though not in the traditional way). James does not offer an oath to guarantee the truth of this letter. He rejects all oaths! In 5:13–18 there is a health wish as James instructs them in how to obtain health through prayer. And then, finally, he sums up the purpose of his letter in 5:19–20. His aim has been to warn sinners of their erroneous ways.

5:13–18 The theme of this section is prayer. Prayer is the form of speech that James commends most highly in his letter. However, James also identifies two other forms of speech which ought to characterize Christians: singing (v. 13) and confession of sins (v. 16). Such proper speech contrasts with the two forms of improper speech identified in the previous section: grumbling (v. 8) and oath-taking (v. 12). In this way, James summarizes his teaching on speech while at the same time extending it to new areas.

5:13 *trouble.* James does not define the nature of the trouble. However, in the course of his letter he has pointed out a variety of troubles facing the church: favoritism (2:1–4), exploitation and litigation (2:5–7; 5:1–6); lack of the physical necessities of life (2:15), slander and cursing (3:9–12; 4:11–12), and community disharmony (3:13–4:3). He has also just alluded to the persecution of the prophets (5:10–11) and to the physical, mental and spiritual suffering of Job (5:11). These are troubles aplenty!

pray. The first response to all these troubles ought to be prayer (see Psalm 30; 50:15; 91:15).

happy / sing. James knows that life is not one unrelenting misery. There are times of joy and these too call for a verbal response—in this case, singing. The Christian church has long been noted for its singing. In his letter to the Roman emperor Trajan describing the Christian sect, Pliny the governor of Bithynia wrote "that they were in the habit of meeting on a certain, fixed day before it was light, when they sang in alternate verses a hymn to Christ as God" (see also 1 Cor. 14:15,26; Eph. 5:19; Col. 3:16).

5:14–15 There is a long tradition of faith healing in the Christian church. Jesus and the apostles healed the sick. In the second century, Irenaeus wrote of healings by means of laying on of hands. In the third century, Tertullian wrote that the Roman emperor Alexander Severus was healed by anointing.

sick. It is one thing to be persecuted, to be hungry, or to fight with other church members. These problems stem from the evil that is in the world. But illness is another matter. It is not something anybody else does to you. Especially in the first century, illness made one feel so vulnerable. What could you do? Where could you go for help? James has an answer to this question.

call the elders. Illness was to be dealt with in the context of the Christian community. The elders—the council that ran the church—were to be called on to minister to the ill person. They had two things to do: to pray over the person and to anoint him or her with oil.

anoint him with oil. When a Jew was ill, he or she first went to a rabbi to be anointed with oil. Oil was used not only for ritual purposes but for cleaning wounds, for paralysis, and for toothaches. In this case, the olive oil is not being used as a medicine but as a part of the healing prayer (see Mark 6:13 and Luke 10:34).

5:15 prayer offered in faith. James has discussed this kind of prayer already (see 1:5–8 and 4:1–3). His point is that "without the life of commitment to God that the prayer expresses, it will be ineffectual. The faith lies in the elders, not in the sick person (about whose faith nothing is said). The elders' faith is critical: If something 'goes wrong' it is they, not the sick person, who bear the onus" (Davids, GNC).

the Lord will raise him up. James is quite clear about the source of the healing. It is not the oil, it is not the laying on of hands by the elders, nor is it even prayer in some sort of magical sense. It is God who heals.

sinned. Traditional Judaism maintained there was a connection between sin and illness: "No sick person is cured of his disease until all his sins are forgiven him" (Babylonian Talmud). Therefore, healing would be a confirmation God had also forgiven the sins that were confessed (see Mark 2:1–12). Though James does not teach an inevitable connection between sin and illness, he suggests that at times this may be the case, much as modern medicine has recognized that illness is often a product of wrong living (psychosomatic illness).

5:16 Therefore. James will summarize his teaching concerning healing and prayer. Public confession and believing prayer are key to what he says.

confess your sins. Confessing your sins to one another removes barriers between people and promotes honesty in the Christian community.

to each other. This is not an action to be taken only when one is ill and then only with the elders. Public confession of sins is for everyone.

powerful and effective. It is not that prayer is an independent force (like magic incantations). Prayer is directed to *God,* who is all-powerful and who works in this world.

5:17–18 Elijah. Though in the story told in 1 Kings 17 and 18 no direct mention is made of Elijah praying, the rabbis taught that the words in 1 Kings 17:1, "whom I serve" (which is translated literally "standing before God") and the words in 1 Kings 18:42, "bent down to the ground," refer to prayer.

a man just like us. Elijah was not a plastic saint more comfortable in another world than this one. He knew depression, despair and doubt just as did the Christians in the church of James' day (see 1 Kings 19). And yet, God answered his prayer in a mighty way. Perhaps James realizes at this point that he could be misinterpreted in what he had said about prayer and be understood to mean that only a special few could pray and expect God to answer. (In verse 15 he mentioned "prayer offered in faith," and he has already said a lot about what real faith is. And in verse 16 it is the prayer of a "righteous man" that avails.) Here he makes it clear that all Christians can pray like this, not just prophets or saints.

5:19–20 James concludes his letter by summarizing its purpose.

wander. Christian truth captivates not only the mind, but one's whole life, including how one lives. This is the point of the book of James. Hence James can speak about wandering from Christian truth, presumably into other styles of living. It is not primarily doctrinal deviation that has concerned James. It is how one lives.

5:20 turns. This word can be translated "converts" when it is applied to unbelievers. "James holds out an assurance of blessing both to the converted and to the converter; the act of conversion is of mutual benefit: the man who is turned from error is thereby delivered from death, and the man who reclaims him experiences himself forgiveness of his sins. It is, of course, assumed that the man who takes it upon himself to reclaim his fellow from error will be conscious of errors of his own for which he too stands in need of forgiveness" (Laws).

cover over a multitude of sins. See 1 Peter 4:8.

COMMENTS
Healing—A Definition

The Gospels depict Jesus as having spent a surprising amount of time healing people. Although, like the author of Job before him, he specifically rejected the theory that sickness was God's way of getting even with sinners (John 9:1–3), he nonetheless seems to have suggested a connection between sickness and sin, almost to have seen sin as a kind of sickness. "Those who are well have no need of a physician, but those who are sick," he said, "I came not to call the righteous but the sinners" (Mark 2:17).

This is entirely compatible, of course, with the Hebrew view of man as a psychosomatic unity, an indivisible amalgam of body and soul whereby if either goes wrong, the other is affected. It is significant also that the Greek verb *sozo* was used in Jesus' day to mean both to save and to heal, and *soter* could signify either savior or physician.

Ever since the time of Jesus, healing has been part of the Christian tradition. In this century it has usually been associated with religious quackery or the lunatic fringe, but as the psychosomatic dimension of disease has come to be taken more and more seriously by medical science it has regained some of its former respectability. How nice for God to have this support at last.

Jesus is reported to have made the blind see and the lame walk, and over the centuries countless miraculous healings have been claimed in his name. For those who prefer not to believe in them, a number of approaches are possible, among them:

1. The idea of miracles is an offense both to man's reason and to his dignity. Thus, a priori, miracles don't happen.

2. Unless there is objective medical evidence to substantiate the claim that a miraculous healing has happened, you can assume it hasn't.

3. If the medical authorities agree that a healing is inexplicable in terms of present scientific knowledge, you can simply ascribe this to the deficiencies of present scientific knowledge.

4. If an otherwise intelligent and honest human being is convinced, despite all arguments to the contrary, that it is God who has healed him, you can assume that his sickness, like its cure, was purely psychological. Whatever that means.

5. The crutches piled high at Lourdes and elsewhere are a monument to human humbug and credulity.

If your approach to this kind of healing is less ideological and more empirical, you can always give it a try. Pray for it. If it's somebody else's healing you're praying for, you can try at the same time laying your hands on him as Jesus sometimes did. If his sickness involves his body as well as his soul, then God may be able to use your inept hands as well as your inept faith to heal him.

If you feel like a fool as you are doing this, don't let it throw you. You are a fool of course, only not a damned fool for a change.

If your prayer isn't answered, this may mean more about you and your prayer than it does about God. Don't try too hard to feel religious, to generate some healing power of your own. Think of yourself (if you have to think of yourself at all) as a rather small-gauge, clogged-up pipe that a little of God's power may be able to filter through if you can just stay loose enough. Tell the one you're praying for to stay loose, too.

If God doesn't seem to be giving you what you ask, maybe he's giving you something else (Frederick Buechner, *Wishful Thinking: A Theological ABC*, New York: Harper and Row, 1973, pp. 35–37).